MW01294329

The Pocket Pierre

by

Pierre Grimes

with

Cathy Wilson

Photos courtesy of stock.xchng (www.sxu.hu)
Drawings by Cathy Wilson
Drawings in *Dialogue Summaries*
by Pierre Grimes

Table of Contents

Foreword

By Cathy Wilson

My son introduced me to Pierre Grimes in 2010. I attended one of the Noetic Society meetings (http://noeticsociety.org/) and saw Pierre at work. I was amazed that a roomful of people would gather together each week to study Plato in such rigorous analysis. During these meetings, Pierre asks someone to present a dream, which he analyzes using the methods in this book. I was fortunate to share one of my own dreams, and the results were surprising and wonderful, an excellent introduction to Pierre's work. You can see videos explaining this work—and observe recordings of dream analyses—at the website above. You will find it well worth it.

Pierre's groundbreaking work, *Philosophical Midwifery, a New Paradigm for Understanding Human Problems and Its Validation,* written with Regina L. Uliana, contains a complete explanation of this powerful method for improving your life. In addition, Pierre has written many other books on the method, which you can find on Amazon.com. My current favorite, which gives a thorough understanding of how the method came to be, is *The Way of The Logos, Volume II, The Reflection,* published in 2011. Like much of Pierre's work, it is written in a delightful dialogue form, and it gives a comprehensive understanding of the method based in philosophy and in logic.

People sometimes puzzle over the words: Philosophical Midwifery (PM). For one thing, most of us associate philosophy with a rather confusing journey into the thought processes of historical and modern philosophers. However, Pierre uses the term to refer to Platonic philosophy. Again, most of us may be baffled as we try to read Plato, not being accustomed to the language nor the logic of the dialogue.

Pierre simplifies it for us. Philosophy in the Platonic tradition is not just a philosopher's way of thinking, but rather it is a careful journey to finding the truth — not a truth based on someone's religion, but the truth in ourselves. In this way, philosophy is closely connected with the spiritual world. Pierre demonstrates that the mind is the pathway to the truth, and thus to the spirit. Although this idea contradicts the modern notion of philosophy, it is reliable and comforting.

And why the term "midwifery"? Not surprising: it's found in Plato, and Pierre uses it to distinguish this work from current psychological methods, which are based on the idea that something is wrong with us, something that a trained professional can fix. PM is based on asking questions in a careful sequence. Anybody can do it (and the workbook included here lets you learn it for yourself). Instead of the idea that something is wrong with us, PM shows that our problems come from early experiences in our life, from which we drew incorrect conclusions. You'll see how that works as you read the book.

And why this book? It's because readers sometimes find the original work a little difficult. At some point, you'll want to get hold of that book and read it for a complete understanding of the method and background. In the meantime, enjoy this user-friendly introduction to the method. It can transform your life, as it has mine.

"Truth radiates from true Being, never does it pass into any other stage, but fills the souls of those who are not strangers to the divine. First, it illuminates those who can participate in her. Second, she brings the depth of perfection to souls. Third, the soul's essence reveals itself as no different from Mind itself."

Welcome to Philosophical Midwifery

There's something you need to know:

You are part of a caring and understandable universe.

When you really get that, then you may also realize that you have many things working for you—in particular, your mind, which constantly communicates with you for your benefit.

The communications from your mind are profound, and they are totally appropriate for you. Even though your mind *can* reach far and wide, it also precisely focuses on what is personally important for you.

In other words,

- o   your choice of goals,
- o   the problems you face,
- o   the daydreams or fantasies you have,
- o   and the dreams that visit you in your sleep—
- o   each and every one of these are like doorways into the richest insights that can help you in your life. These insights show us that every day, your mind is working for your good in a generous and understandable way.

In a world that seems chaotic and sometimes dark, it may be hard to believe in a kind universe working for your good, in a mind that is working diligently to help you, so we will show you proof for this kind of thinking. And we will demonstrate that the problems that you have are problems you *should* have, and that you can solve them, and that solving your problems is maybe the most important thing you can do for yourself, because it will bring you to a higher and more personally significant kind of life.

Problems

Most of us think of our problems as painful and negative. Here we will define problems in a new way and describe what problems are really like. We will trace the beginnings of your problems to things you *learned,* and discover why you believed and accepted

6

these things as true. This new way of looking at problems will give us a method for solving them— what we call Philosophical Midwifery—and this whole process will help us see that the universe is indeed beneficial and intelligible, and so is your life.

Why Do We Have Problems Anyway?

The main source of many of our problems is a particular kind of false belief that we can call *pathologos,* which roughly means a belief that is "sick" or false. That is, a pathologos is a false belief, something that is learned—but not taught (more about this later: it is a critical part of Philosophical Midwifery). It is something you have accepted as true about yourself and your reality, but it conflicts with your best good and with reaching your highest goals--and causes all sorts of difficulty for you—so it causes much of the chaos you may experience.

Philosophical Midwifery is the method for discovering the pathologos—what it is, what it's like, where it came from, how we maintain it in our lives, how we transmit it to others—and how we can get rid of it. We use the term *pathologos* to distinguish this unique idea from other psychological terms, which often point to so-called character flaws—or even sins— in ourselves rather than false ideas that we can identify and bring to an end.

The pathologos, this false belief, is very strange because we rarely suspect it even exists, even though we absolutely accept it as true. When finally we can see it for what it is, it can be compared to a *psychic parasite* that infects by transmitting delusions to its host, delusions which disguise what it really *is*. Whenever something threatens to reveal it, it vigorously undermines the truth to protect itself.

The pathologos is like a parasite because it drains us of our vitality, turning us away from our highest goals and often causing us serious problems. It is psychic because it creates and sustains delusions. And it functions like a carrier of disease because, sadly, it passes itself—and its conditions—on to the family or clan.

Philosophical Midwifery identifies and describes the pathologos. It may seem difficult to understand at first, but you'll find your way as we explain it here.

The Nature of the Pathologos

What is a pathologos like?

Here we'll see what it's like, take a look at its cycles in your life and its links to other beliefs, its relation to your self-image, its power to counter-attack, and finally, we'll discuss how to remove it!

When we are young, we witness powerful scenes which lead us to make false conclusions about ourselves and our reality. These scenes lead us to make conclusions which we take as absolutely true and indisputable. No one actually *taught* us these conclusions; that is, no one taught them aloud, but instead, powerful situations taught us the pathologos.

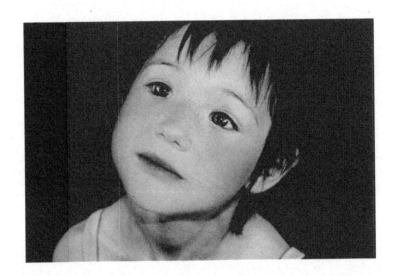

Every pathologos begins in a unique circumstance in our past, but all share the same form or structure. Philosophical Midwifery provides questions that can reveal the pathologos which came from a particular scene from our youth. These questions begin in the present, with problems we are having right now, which then lead us to find out and understand what created the pathologos.

The pathologos functions as a monad, or a single entity. In other words, it's not a complex of difficult problems; it's *one* kind of pattern that shows up in various circumstances in our lives, almost as if it sees itself again and again. When we learn to recognize the pathologos, we can easily see how it manifests in our problems every day.

The scenes that produce a pathologos are always dramatic; all the scenes fit together in a drama. Within each scene there is:

- some action,
- content (or words, or "logos"),
- and an accompanying state of mind.

The state of mind is the effect the drama has on you. This effect is deep and long-reaching. Once you accept a pathologos, it plays itself out in your life over and over again, so it keeps reappearing in cycles. When at last you begin to notice these cycles and become familiar with them, you can anticipate and understand why sometimes they are incredibly intense, while other times, less so. You will also notice that the cycles show up as harmful patterns in your life—something we all relate to!

And once you understand a pathologos, you can see how your pathologos problems all link together, forming patterns that you can actually chart into a network and see the connections between the various problems connected with it. Then, as you understand the origins of a pathologos, you can test out *solutions* to it in various situations in your life. Indeed, with this work, you can actually stop the destructive patterns that have held you back in life, even such difficulties as addiction.

The Network of the Pathologos

Each pathologos is linked to others in a network of beliefs, which connect together like the teeth of meshing gears.

Understanding how one pathologos links with another, we see their mutual connections, and can begin to track how the pathologos has developed, how it works. As we go along, we begin to see the pathologos more and more clearly, defining it more and more. Soon we can put into words the actual message of a pathologos, following how the meaning of the message developed over our lives, so we can also see how the false belief developed over our lives—and brought us to our current state.

The pathologos shapes itself over the years until it forms our basic image of ourselves. It becomes the mask, or the persona, that is our way of being in the world. We develop the pathologos and our persona (the mask) at the same time, and these bring about all our problems in life. Philosophical Midwifery can help us see these things for what they really are, and then we can overcome our problems.

Unfortunately, while we work to surface the pathologos, to understand how it is maintained, and to understand how to resolve it, the pathologos launches an unusual defense mechanism, the *counter-attack*, to prevent its removal. Remember that the pathologos is a potent belief we received early in life, and one of its key functions is to undermine any work that might remove it.

We may reach good conclusions with our work in Philosophical Midwifery—and then immediately we begin to doubt the conclusions, we question the method, and our minds fill with doubt and disbelief. When we experience this flood of doubt, we may want to throw away all that good work, but it will be more helpful to carefully examine each doubt and each contrary argument, because they fit together into the *defense* of the pathologos, which we may experience as loyalty to our old beliefs or as an attack against their new way of understanding. Later in the book, we will examine the counter-attack, including examples, in detail.

How the Pathologos Gets Passed On

A pathologos affects your entire life, and it can be traced through generations, too. It can be carried through the generations because it teaches a supposedly ideal way of being which, though unspoken, is imitated by children from their parents. How does this imitation happen? To know this, we need to understand *how* we learn it when we are young.

There are, of course, different ways of learning things. We learn a language in different ways than we learn to ride a bicycle. To learn the pathologos, we must become convinced that a particular belief is true—not just any belief, but a basic belief about our own worthiness and about our basic reality. When we accept a pathologos, we have been totally convinced by someone else that we are ignorant about our very being and deluded about what we think is real. This person convinces us that they know us better than we know ourselves, so they know what's real even though we don't.

Someone must have been very convincing, and that can only have happened if someone appeared as a *knower* with such skill that he became idealized in our minds, so that through a drama with that person, we totally accepted their message, totally believed it.

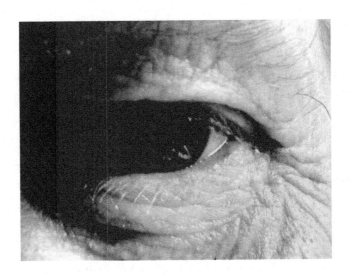

This word is very important, a *knower*. You'll recognize right away what this person is like. He becomes an unquestioned *ideal* in the drama, so that we feel we must imitate him, and indeed, he sets the standard for knowing what is true and real. Although this whole set-up seems pretty clear, a further explanation will help us understand the power of the learning.

When one person transmits a belief to another person, it requires a special situation—a unique kind of situation. Several factors must be in place for a pathologos to be transmitted. For one thing, we must be young when it happens, because only an open and receptive child can accept such a thing. Then the drama can only be convincing if *we* are the object of the lesson—the only person in the audience, as it were. Those playing roles in the drama are only convincing if we totally believe that they really know us well and they understand our reality.

Still, none if it would work unless we believe that the actors are working for our benefit. When these factors come together, the entire presentation becomes an ideal that we feel compelled to imitate in our lives. Even though the drama is powerful, no one actually tells us outright we must believe, so we are left to make our own conclusions.

How does each of these elements produce the pathologos? And why is it so difficult to free ourselves of the pathologos?

Before a situation can turn into a pathologos, certain factors must be present. To begin with, the players must be people who are significant to us, people with power over us, and at the same time, we must be in a particularly sensitive and open state of mind to make the conclusions of a pathologos. Such situations are unusual, not typical for day-to-day family life.

When we are young, it goes without saying that we learn most things within our family. So, in the family, we learn from our parents the false beliefs of the family and clan. Even though these beliefs are not usually true and are often harmful, families still pass them down from parents to child. If you think for just a moment, you can probably name a few you've noticed in your own family. We maintain these beliefs inside the family, within the walls of our homes. We've all heard the saying, "Your home is your castle," and while this is usually taken as positive, it also can be negative, because in the home, the parents rule with a strange and powerful authority. From these authorities, with these authorities, we learn our pathologos.

How did the authorities—our parents, our guardians—gain such power to convince us of something so fundamental as the nature of who we are? As we grow up, there are plenty of things we learn without imitating those who teach us. For us to have idealized a person into something so supreme that we must imitate them is pretty strange, but it

18

becomes far more strange when we realize that what we learn from them becomes the standard for *everything* we know from then on.

Think of it this way. When someone breaks clear from the everydayness of his life, it's easy to see when he does it. It's obvious when someone starts to play an authority role and tries to convince us that what they are saying is true.

Sometimes we do this ourselves, taking on the role of the *knower*, but right when we're doing it, we usually know that some people won't agree with us. We realize that not many people really care what we think, unless what we are saying challenges their own thinking. Most of the time, we don't find many situations where we can share our most fundamental beliefs with other people. And when we do, we can't be sure they'll treat our beliefs with much respect.

But even with all these drawbacks, most of us love to play the *knower*. We like it because there's something so inspirational about playing the knower role. We feel proud, noble, and important; the experience is usually intense enough to make us try it out with new people if the first ones don't agree with us.

Realizing that there are very few times when we can express what is most important to us, the deep beliefs we took on when we were little, we usually don't say them out loud. We rarely express these deep beliefs to other people, and so our silence makes us strangers to ourselves. We are not talking about dogma or beliefs that we've learned from someone else teaching us, but rather our deepest beliefs about ourselves and how we fit in the world. Most of us are pretty much unaware of how strongly we hold onto these basic beliefs about ourselves, and although we may voice various beliefs we hear from *others*, we usually don't articulate what we deeply believe about ourselves. In the same way, we are only dimly aware that we have come to powerful personal conclusions about the way we experience reality. What may be even more surprising is that we jealously guard our strong opinions about how we are supposed to act and appear in this reality we experience.

Even though we rarely express these things, they influence *everything* in our lives, so it's no surprise that when we find ourselves in situations where we can express what we believe and feel about life, we jump on the opportunity. Even if we take the opportunity to express ourselves, we can't be sure that people will accept what we say. But there is one receptive audience who *will* listen and care about what we say. This audience will almost never oppose us or offer counter arguments.

This audience is the family—in particular, our children.

With our children, with the young ones in our care, we express our deepest concerns. Whether we realize it or not, we arrange special times for them to learn about our worries and beliefs. To our children, we present what's most important to us. We feel justified—even obligated—to communicate our beliefs to them, and we do it with sincerity and power because we believe we are doing it for their benefit. In these special times and circumstances, the *knower* in us emerges, and our children remember these times because we, the parents and guardians, have made sure of it.

In these situations, children believe with all their hearts that their parents are really knowers, and that they care enough to share their knowledge with the young ones. In these special moments, the parents appear authoritarian, certain, powerful, and totally in control. Thus they are believable, and when children believe them, then they are accepted as members of the family and clan.

There's no way for the young to reject these beliefs. Doing that would be rejecting the parents as the caring and all-powerful beings that they are to little ones. Young children can only know the world inside their families. They have nothing to contrast it with, so it is unthinkable to reject what the parents offer. If somehow a child could do it, parents would be immediately stripped of their authority and power. If children and parents were somehow made equal, it follow that there wouldn't even be a need for the parents at all. Losing that relationship would be enough to destroy a young, immature child. Indeed, many of us could hardly endure it as grownups.

Of course, to secure the message of the drama, the players always pay careful attention to their audience. They especially make sure that they show themselves in the best light, because they know the message may not be believed if the performance is not taken as real. In these dramas, the young child is in awe of the power of those in the drama and impressed by the force of the moment. From our parents, those we believe who know us best, we learn something that we believe must be true — true in a personal way.

When our parents share these beliefs with us, we enter into those beliefs with them and take them for our own. As they reveal what they themselves believe, we share in their reality at the same time as we share in their ways of thinking. The content of the pathologos belief may be partially verbal, but the entire meaning comes across from the authorities (the parents), in their manner, and in the situation itself.

When we are young, we are impressed by the appearance of sincerity, and we believe the parents' message because it seems so real to us. Normal, everyday life is different than a pathologos scene, so when our parents, who are intimately woven into our lives, play out such a scene, the moment takes on great significance. We feel they are not only sincere, but that they are the very image of beauty and truth. When we perceive this beauty, as children, we equate it with truth, because it is generally known that beauty in itself can be persuasive. Beauty carries a sense of truth about it, so that something may feel as if it *should* be that way. Thus beauty plays a central role in the development of our problems, but we may not always be aware of it.

When we are recovering from our pathologos, we often recall that our parents never seemed so forthright, so decisive, so much themselves, as when they were acting out the pathologos, and so we often do see beauty there. As adults, we know that beauty is not a sure sign of the presence of truth, but as children, we usually had not learned that sad lesson.

Learning the pathologos also reveals to us a social reality that we had not thought of before. When we were little, we accepted that reality, and so we began to participate in it. Accepting this reality, this belief, this new learning, creates a bridge between the pathologos scene and our environment. The belief helps us explain to ourselves much of what has been happening around us, including a kind of explanation for many things in the household that previously puzzled us. With this new belief, through the belief, the puzzles become clear. We glimpse why our parents feel what they do, say what they say, and are the way they are. We intuitively grasp how our home environment fits into the pathologos.

Each part of our environment begins to make sense to us. Each part plays out its given role, and each part fits together in a unity that makes the whole thing intelligible and even necessary. We accept this as the way things are, we realize that this is the way things *have* to be, and we accept that our parents will use this to justify their words and deeds. Even as little children, we also sense that something is wrong with all this, but we go along and accept it, and this causes pain for us. That pain becomes the root cause of our anger. It may be "just the way things are," but we know it is not just.

Thus, the pathologos is the key piece to a puzzle that brings a certain order to everything that goes on around us. We can call this the *milieu*.

The pathologos is the keystone that fits everything together, with the image of "the way things are." And oddly, this brings a sense of justification to the pathologos. In order for us to believe it, the pathologos demands this sense of justification, because the moment it is no longer felt to be "just," it dissolves. As long as it goes unchallenged, it seems formidable and great.

Through the pathologos, we receive and accept our roles in the family, we take on certain duties, and we gain status and eventually confer status on others. The pathologos thus becomes the source of authority in the household, and we staunchly defend it because the pathologos scene presents it as if it possesses or exhibits some kind of greatness. The pathologos continues to exist only as long as the image of greatness is taken to be real and as long as we believe this reality to be just.

The lesson we learn from the pathologos has a vast influence on us without our being aware of it. Whatever and however the parents reveal themselves becomes the ideal that the child imitates. The power of the lesson extends into the inner life of our dreams and fantasies. It shapes our attitudes and our reactions to our reality.

Clearly then, the pathologos became the ideal to which we unknowingly molded ourselves. The ideal is stamped into our minds as the highest way of being which we *must* imitate. Behind our desire to imitate is the inner urge to become like what was presented to us in the pathologos, because we perceive it as greatness. We want to be great, as the pathologos belief taught us.

In fact, greatness and imitation of it are the conditions for the pathologos. The gestures, expressions, and attitudes displayed at that moment are taken on and become part of ourselves. It is as if the psyche were a strange, blind master craftsman who could transform himself by adapting another person's mask and making it his own, all the while remaining unaware that he did it. These masks, our persona, stay in place for a lifetime, and in turn, we pass them on to our children. We do not recognize that these masks trap us into patterns of behavior that distress and bewilder us. Nor do we see the destruction of our highest ideals which results from these simple scenes from our childhood.

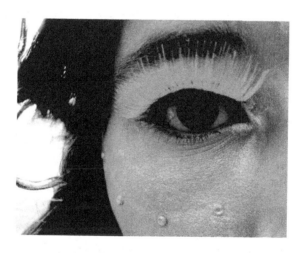

Once we think about it, we do realize that our repetitive behavior, the patterns we keep repeating in our lives, had to come from somewhere, and they keep us trapped with no chance to improve ourselves. We have imitated these patterns from someplace outside ourselves. Imitating, becoming like the model, striving to be accepted as someone or something—all that comes from a powerful urge to become like what we accept as ideal or great.

The parents establish themselves as *knowers;* they present a powerful image of *knowing,* and in this way they establish their authority. Against this image, imbued with beauty and justice, we compare everything in our lives. The beliefs of the pathologos have a particular combination of virtues or qualities; each combination is particular in itself, and identifying these qualities helps us understand that particular pathologos. This combination of qualities becomes the ideal for the family, for the group. The standards of behavior within the family, or the signs of being accepted within the family, all revolve around these qualities. All members know what this standard is, and they measure up to it, or not—but everyone knows what the standard is, and they settle into their roles in the family based on that standard. Without the powerful urge to imitate the ideal, there would be no pathologos, for the urge is more fundamental and more primitive than desire. The unique model presented in the pathologos scene sets the standard, the ideal.

If parents only behave in this unique way under circumstances that are unusual and rare, then that rare event intensifies, becoming even more important and significant. The less the parents reveal of themselves, the more the need for that rare behavior. And the more they reveal themselves, the more

28

important it will be to discover the reason for the repeated behavior. However, if the parents have a wide range of revealing themselves, then any single pathologos event will have less of an impact.

If a child were to reject the pathologos message, it would mean calling into question the integrity of his parents, who are sincere and beautiful to the child. This would make it impossible to continue in the family structure the way we did before. It takes huge courage and understanding to challenge the pathologos, even among the mature. Some do return to their parents and families and challenge the pathologos, and in these cases, it takes an unusual level of commitment and courage for mature adults. It would be impossible for the young to do this.

At what age does the pathologos take hold the most powerfully? Clearly, it has to be at a young age when the parents still retain their image of ultimate authority, in dependent relationships, which just about always means in early childhood. These early scenes always include the sacrifice of what we think is real from our own experience. The pathologos drama absolutely must conceal from the child that the actors are acting out an act, that it isn't real. Otherwise the child could never accept the pathologos belief and reject his own perception of reality.

There are only two possibilities: accept the act and performers as real, or reject the whole thing as just an act. In accepting the drama as real, and modeling ourselves on it because we think it is a higher or better way, we actually become less than ourselves, altering our experiences to fit a belief that goes with the drama. As long as this structure stays in place, it maintains the pathologos.

How do our parents know when to act out this tragic drama? It almost always has to take place when the child is in an open and exploring state of mind. When we are young, when our state of mind is usually free, open, with natural integrity, and when we are in this innocent and open state, we are sadly open to the pathologos. In this natural state, we face others directly, with equality. We accept them for what they are or what they seem to be. It is natural for a child to expect others to be in the same state as they are, to be open, direct, and honest. From such states of mind, we discover what is most our own. This openness gives us access into our world, but it also gives us passageway into another's, and this open state becomes the doorway into the pathologos.

There are times when parents allow the young child to remain in its sincerity and openness, but sooner or later, parents impose their concerns—and the pathologos—on the child. There are few parents who avoid doing this. If parents could, they would be giving their child the greatest gift: a chance to become independent of the parents and perhaps to become different from them. It would mean allowing the child to pursue goals that give nothing to the parents and which would make the parents secondary in the child's life. Yet in the long run, is that not what parents would wish for: a child who grows up into a unique and independent self?

Here is a simple example of how a pathologos might work. What if children were treated as though they were doing something bad every time they were caught absorbed in a private reflection or personally satisfying activity? And suppose that children were only praised when doing some domestic chore or practical task. Would these children conclude that being practical, or that serving the family, escapes criticism and conflict?

If children are repeatedly told that they should do everything they can for the parents and for the family, are they likely to grow up feeling that being by and for oneself is wrong and selfish? Wouldn't such children eventually avoid being introspective and speculative about life? They might conclude that it's better to lower your expectations than to waste your efforts seeking an unobtainable idea. Soon practical goals stand in for the ideal, and compromise becomes the solution to everything, and in this process, a noble being is transformed into a shadow of himself, and freedom becomes only a faint memory.

Sadly, the very state of openness that we say we love in children is a condition that most parents cannot allow to continue, because it challenges the pathologos and threatens its very existence. No doubt parents intuit that a child's openness will be inhibited by imposing adult beliefs on him, but they also realize that allowing the child to remain open will invalidate their own reality. They would rather inhibit the child's personal development than challenge or destroy their own pathologos. Perhaps the imposition of the belief doesn't directly address a child's state of openness, but the content of the belief always affects it and is the object of the lesson: to put aside your personal experience of the world in favor of the parents' beliefs.

There are many subtle ways that family members communicate that they have accepted this primitive social contract. By accepting it, they become members of the family, clan or tradition and can participate in its dramas of acceptance or rejection, reward or punishment. It defines the family members' roles, sets up various family procedures, and determines the kinds of relationships that will be allowed within the family and outside it, too. The pathologos sets the stage for the skillful use of benefits, praise, love, intimidations, humiliations, exile, and coercion to maintain the group, since the pathologos keeps in place a way of being, controlling the family's states of mind to keep them firmly within the milieu, producing an emotional climate that supports the dramas of the pathologos.

The more strongly the pathologos dominates the family milieu, the more difficult it is for any member to separate from it, because if the milieu is challenged, the parents may retaliate with angry, scornful and possibly hostile acts on the child who doesn't accept the way the family functions. The pathologos is always introduced as the rational, normal view of the world. It does *appear* rational. In fact, it appears as if it were an exception to the milieu, because in the face of all difficulties brought about by the pathologos, the parents will appear as caring and rational beings, while in reality, the pathologos removes their ability to truly care for and nurture their child.

Many people find it difficult to believe that the pathologos can account for so much of the craziness in the family. When people realize that they must separate from the pathologos, in order to become their healthy selves, they often go into crisis when they realize they also must separate from the family. At this point, many people try to think of all the good points of the pathologos and even defend it, which all seem safer than trusting one's own experience of the world. Leaving the pathologos—and usually the family—may leave a person with a profound sense of emptiness, perhaps a deep bitterness, and a sense of isolation. These negative feelings, though, are balanced with the great gift of becoming your own person, a mature self in a world you can perceive clearly yourself.

We are not saying that children should be left to grow up without learning how to live and act within the family. Of course, there should be models and ideals to prepare them for life. But when they adopt models which come from pathologos scenes, then it follows that the models are pathological: they are unhealthy and toxic. Children do not possess the ability to discriminate between healthy models and pathological ones, so in families dominated by the pathologos (and sadly, this means most families), they accept the unhealthy model. The model we accept as a child binds us to an image, and that bond becomes a sign of our love for our parents.

The root of every pathologos is modeling ourselves after our parents, who appeared to be *knowers* in the early pathologos scenes. We continue to preserve that image of the parents as powerful knowers, and then we perpetuate that image in our own lives.

Why would we extend an unhealthy belief system into adulthood? It is because every pathologos presents within itself a model of caring and love. At the moment of the pathologos scene, we believe that our parents are giving us their loving attention and highest regard, sharing with us their vision of what they regard as most important, most real. But what we didn't know was that we would absorb it as our own model of caring, loving and knowing—and that it wasn't loving at all.

Then, when we are adults, we are drawn to those around us who play similar roles to the figures in our past, and we continue acting in roles similar to what we absorbed in the pathologos scene. Unless we recognize that we are acting out a pathologos role in these dramas, we will likely keep acting them out, usually with tragic outcomes. There is a power to these relationships that echo the ones we learned in the pathologos scene. We are strongly attracted to such relationships and often display an intense loyalty to keeping them alive. They remind us of the early conflicts in the pathologos scene in which we wrongly believed to be shared moments of genuine intimacy.

So when someone comes along and plays a role similar to those in the pathologos scenes, we are vulnerable and may think we are receiving love while we are actually playing out another version of the pathologos drama. It's inevitable, when we do this, that our pathologos will manifest itself, but often we are willing to pay a very high price for our loyalty to the pathologos as we devote ourselves to the new relationship. It doesn't take long for love to be overshadowed by another version of the pathologos drama, and then chaos enters the relationship.

As we consider the pathologos, we should remember that in the strict sense, the family does *not* impose or force a particular belief on its members, not directly. Instead the child comes to a conclusion, a strange, wordless conclusion that tries to make sense of the pathologos-producing scene. As children, we draw these conclusions ourselves, but not because someone taught us verbally. These are non-verbal conclusions we draw from the pathologos scenes.

We are learning all the time, especially as children, even though we are not being *taught*. From our earliest days, we try to make sense of the world around us, and throughout our lives, we draw conclusions from our experiences. In this way, children learn from these scenes that parents have power and authority over them. The child submits, the limits are set, and a new reality sets in. Now the child can survive as a member of the family, with new roles and a new identity.

This all seems so irresistible. Why don't children reject the drama, call it a fiction, reject it as unjust? Why didn't we remain in our own reality instead of accepting the incorrect reality of the pathologos? Why didn't we just say what was going on? Were we afraid of retaliation, of punishment? Of course, it would have taken a great deal of courage to object to the drama, but lack of courage doesn't explain it.

It may help to remember a few things. First, we know that in every scene, there was no justification for the parents to play out their drama as they did, and also, in the beginning of every pathologos scene, the child is in a good state of mind. So the child can recall nothing that could justify the drama. Prior to the drama, so far as the child is concerned, nothing particular is going on, nothing that could justify the drama. In these scenes, something affects the parents so much that they leave everyday normality and reveal what matters most to them in a powerful way. The parents have reached "the end of their tether" and act out a drama detached from normality.

The child has to notice what it took for the parents to leave their normal state of mind. The parents reached their limit; they couldn't go any further; so they reveal to the child what can happen if he or she crosses that line. The child has to ask himself, in one way or another, "If they get this upset for *that*, well, what would they do if I challenged the truth of all that? If challenging *that* challenges their very being, if it takes them *that* far, then what would they do if I dared to challenge, doubt or even reject the truth they are communicating?"

At least, in the pathologos drama, the parents seem that they cannot go any further. But *can* they take any more? Could they go further? Could the child risk playing the next card? Everything would change if the drama were challenged. If any drama is challenged, it redefines the parameters of the drama, and then the way of life changes, too. Well, the child must decide. The parents have reached their limit. If the child cannot confront them about it, then he accepts the limits of the drama. The parents establish the limits; when the child accepts them and justifies them, it becomes the pathologos.

An interesting ratio happens here, a symbolic ratio. It is as if the child asks, "If doing nothing caused that much of a reaction, what would happen to them—

and to me—if I challenged it all?" Children know that they don't have much experience in life, so children almost always accept the views of the parents. It is as if the child reasons that these parents know far more than he does, something beyond his comprehension, something that gives them the right to insist that their reality is truer than the child's. In accepting all of that, in assuming it is true, the child accepts that his vision of reality is profoundly flawed. With that acceptance, the parent's views gain priority over everything else. And what happens to a child's own views and own way of being? It loses all significance, so the child loses the belief in his own reality. As the drama grows over time, as it gains power and credibility, the child's way of being becomes submerged, and he is left only with a role to play in the family drama, becoming a shadow of his former self.

When this happens, the child loses his connection with what had great meaning for him before. Instead, he forgets it and denies it. And what replaces it? It is his role in the drama, which grows in its feeling of seriousness until it comes to feel deeply authentic.

Dialogue Summaries

It will be easier to understand the whole process if we can look in on a couple of actual dialogues. Over the 25 years of this work, I've midwifed thousands of these talks, estimating from my old appointment calendars, because I keep no other records of the talks. Most of them have been audio-taped, and some more recent ones are video-taped.

The talks we will read here come from volunteers from the Noetic Society. Many members volunteered tapes of their talks, and I simply chose the first two. Because the talks took place many years ago, the volunteers would not have known, at the time, that these recorded talks would someday be used in this book.

We had the tapes transcribed, and I made a summary of each talk. Then, going through the tapes, I summarized each five-minute interval of the dialogue. For each of these intervals, we included representative quotes. Each talk took about an hour and a half in real time.

During each session, we use a blackboard to outline the development of the dialogue. In this way, the person can observe visually what is being said aloud, reflecting on his words and thoughts and reflecting on similarities between the present situation and the past scenes. I encourage midwives to use the blackboard, because it is a simple way to fix the person's mind on the development of their thought, to keep the issue before them, and give a simple way they face their own thought without someone else reminding them or interpreting the thoughts. However, when there's no blackboard, I always make detailed notes of the talk, which become the property of the person.

Before we begin, here's a brief comment on my choice of words such as "midwifery" and "pregnant." I chose these to point out that Philosophical Midwifery is not psychotherapy or treatment for mental health issues.

These sessions will seem different in many ways, but they reflect basic attitudes toward our problems: either we believe we understand and are somewhat shocked that we really don't; or we believe we can't understand and are surprised to discover that we do, after all, understand. As you read these dialogues, you will notice how difficult it is for the person to hold onto the logical conclusions that emerge, how often he or she falls back into the pathologos. Seeing this is helpful as we work with our own pathologos and help others midwife theirs.

You will note that these dialogues are experiences of older children; however, they reveal pathologos problems that began earlier in the subjects' lives.

Anna

At the time of this dialogue, Anna was a single, 25-year-old graduate student in political science. She had been exploring her blocks for about two years before this talk, and she had no psychotherapeutic experience before these talks. Her father was a college graduate and had been a flight instructor in the military. Her mother and sister were housewives and businesswomen, and her brother was a graduate student.

Anna is talking about a statistics textbook she'd been studying. She recalls what she said to herself when she got discouraged: "Oh, you've already read this before, just go on, skip it." When she said this to herself, she was picking at her face. She continues, "You always skip it, but when you need to remember it, you don't," adding, "No! Go back and study it! Why do I have to go through such pain with this? It's embarrassing to recognize I don't know this stuff."

She makes a comment which counts as an answer to her question: "I have to study the problem if I am going to say I understand it."

Returning to the question, "Why do I have to go through such pain?" she answers, "Because I deserve it." Questioned further about deserving it, she remarks that since she didn't study it before, she deserves to be punished; she needs to be punished, "because I didn't learn it originally." Reflecting on what she just said, she realizes something strange in what she's saying, and sees that if she had learned it originally, she could have avoided all these difficulties.

This leads her to admit, "I feel very discouraged that I hadn't learned it originally." She recognizes that this line of thought fits into a pattern "for everything I get into." She tells herself, "I don't learn what I set out to learn originally. I don't get into it," and acknowledges that this happens whether she studies it before or not.

Yet she blames herself for not knowing it, since "I should've studied this before. When I did have the time, I wasted it." Continuing to reflect in this way, she comes up with an apparent solution: "Get through it. Then you can study afterwards." She reports, however, that this attitude of "get through it" is present whether she studies it originally or tries to learn it later.

When she does study, she tells herself, "I have to hurry up."

"Otherwise," the midwife interjects, "you might understand it."

"Oh, it's a waste of time to understand," Anna insists. "Just get through it."

She adds that every time she takes a test, she did not understand, so she concludes, "It's a waste of time. Just get through it." She anticipates being caught and confronted with partial understanding. "Someone will always catch me on something I didn't see," she says, "They'll say, 'Why didn't you see that [understand that] before?'"

Then she recalls a specific occasion when she was in the eighth grade and had to have a math assignment done for the following day. She saw she couldn't do it, and feared that if the teacher were to discover how little she knew, she would be put back a grade in school. Her solution: "I have to bluff."

Her mother's solution: "Don't worry about it. You are an average student."

Anna concludes, "So I don't have to understand it."

She recalls asking her father for help, but she knew that while he could solve the simpler word problems assigned for homework, he could never explain to her how he did them. She would watch him, knowing that she wasn't learning, and say to herself, "I'm not going to be able to understand it." After another unsuccessful tutoring session with her father, she decided the best way to prepare for the math test would be to memorize the problems in the text and to apply them to word problems in the test that seemed similar.

"So I used to say, 'Well, I'm not very good at word problems.' My mother would say, 'Well I wasn't very good, either,' and my dad would say, 'Well, I'm not that great either.'" So Anna concludes, "Gee, if they got by, why should I work 'em out?"

Anna doesn't seem to see the implications of these remarks. She insists that she still cannot understand word problems. I ask her, "Do you have an example of something you've studied and understood?"

She replies, "I don't have anything I recall that I've understood with my dad." She agrees that the only thing she learned was to "just get through it" and not reflect on it. She then agrees that no one in her family, including herself, was interested in understanding.

I ask her to recall with more detail the problem of her present study scene. She recalls that for the 30 minutes before getting stuck, she had comprehended the text just fine, but when she reached a part of the text she thought was important, she said to herself, "Oh, you've read this before. Go on, skip it," and then she would return to it, but skip it again, over and over. Then she says, "I was picking [my face] and that was distracting."

I asked, "What would happen to the family teaching if you could get through that paragraph?"

"No. It couldn't happen—I mean," she said thoughtfully, "I could make it through the paragraph and feel good."

A few moments later, she forgets that she ever made that comment. "I could never understand word problems," she says. She remembers that she would get discouraged, unsuccessfully trying to solve math problems, and then go to her father, and that's when he tutored her—when she was discouraged. She says, "They [parents] were never interested [in genuinely helping her gain mastery in math or anything else]." She makes a connection between her present problem and the past: when discouraged, she feels "obligated to talk to somebody about it."

Anna recalls at some length a recent example of getting caught in a bluff when she offered an idea to her supervisors, but since she hadn't understood it herself, they just dismissed it. She remarks, "Right after that I said, 'Well, you couldn't have thought of any ideas yourself anyway!'"

Then, reflecting, she says that bluffing and just "getting through it" at least avoids the emotional turmoil of understanding, because whenever she thinks of a new idea, "I'm scared every time" to share the new idea with someone else, so "I wipe them [the ideas] out even before I can present them, or get into them."

After discussing how this is similar to the early math scenes, I asked her to reflect on the fact that she understood her statistics text till she reached a key passage. She insists that she can't remember further details about this, but after a moment, she says that she had recognized that the passage was very important; she saw, "I had to kind of keep that idea in mind, to see how it developed." After some reflection, she saw that doing that, keeping it in mind, would violate the family's "just get through it" advice.

Anna then volunteers another present scene when she was upset because her supervisor asked her to learn something in a short time and discuss it with others. She explained that doing that sharply contrasts her idea of understanding with bluffing. "Understanding, it takes time, relaxation and not being pressed to get through it." She adds, about bluffing, "I get praise for getting through it. I get away with it."

"Suppose," I said, "that you were close to understanding it and panicked, and therefore got into an emotional state because the family teaching is 'Thou Shalt Not Understand'?"

She acknowledges that she does panic, saying, "I get scared at the implication of what I see," and recalls that at such moments, she enters into what she calls fantasy. When she saw the importance of the section in the statistics text, she recalls that she fantasized about success: "Oh, I could go into computers if I understood this."

"You do understand it, don't you?" I asked. "Is that when the fantasies begin?"

"Oh, that's the part I forgot," she says, surprised.

She suddenly realizes that she skipped the paragraph because she did understand it after all. "I started fantasizing then," she says. Yet after seeing this, she has trouble holding onto it and says, as if correcting herself, "No, you don't understand it. You didn't read the paragraph."

I asked her what it would mean to understand the rest of the paragraph.

"Why, I didn't need to read it any further because I knew where the paragraph was going." At the same moment, she finds herself in a quandary. "I know I haven't worked hard enough. It came too quick." She warns herself, "You better check on it." Then she adds, "Confusion starts coming up and I start getting worried."

She reports that she had the insight just before she began to fantasize. "I read the first three lines; saw where it was going," and that made her feel good. But then, "I get scared because I hadn't read the whole paragraph." Confusion and worry set in, so she stops herself and starts all over from the beginning. "It's like I deny what I saw, and I have to go back and forth through it again, because it was too soon, I always see things too soon, and I blame myself for seeing."

"What do you mean?" I ask.

"It's like I deny what I saw, and I have to go back and work through it again." She justifies this, "because it was too soon. I always see things too soon, and I blame myself for seeing."

"What does that mean?" I ask.

When she feels good about seeing or learning, "I'll go into fantasies, and those aren't real." She daydreams about changing careers, but it ends when she tells herself she could never do that kind of work. However, she is also aware that in her moment of understanding, she is already successfully doing the kind of work that is in her fantasy. She realizes that she has to punish herself for even having the fantasy of success and all it entails, since, she agrees, success is her way out of the family.

I continue to ask questions until she realizes that she doesn't need to call her reflections (on a new career) a fantasy, since she is actually dealing with the consequences of her own understanding, and she recognizes that by labeling this a fantasy, she dismisses it instead of seeing that it could be real, and that it is real.

"Why do you go through such pain?" I ask.

"I'm stuck, that's what I'd say."

Then she acknowledges that she has seen some connections through the dialogue.

I ask her to study the book again and see how much of this experience confirms this talk, and to be particularly watchful when the fantasies occur and for the feelings that accompany the fantasies.

Charlie

At the time of this dialogue, Charlie was a married, 35-year-old college graduate pursuing his goal to be a writer. Like many writers, he had been experiencing blocks to his goals; in his case, it had been two years. He had had no prior psychotherapy. His father was a medical technician, his mother was a housewife, and his three sisters were housewives.

After first stating his goal of being a writer, Charlie mentions that he is facing some practical financial problems. Then he says, "I want to write literature, and I want to write stories." He says, "The book I'm writing now is becoming extremely involved, and I love it!"

But he has a recurring inner dialogue that is bothering him. "Well, you are going to do that book, but maybe you should spend your time looking for a job, you know?" and "Maybe you should spend your time writing something you can get paid for." Finally, "Besides that, I have headaches a lot."

"Tell me more about your headaches," I said.

He talked about a fantasy he had on the way to coming to the talk, where he pictured himself walking out without even talking. He says he knows he should specify the problem he has in pursuing his goals, but he says, "I'm not doing it," adding, "I'm unable to move." He adds, "I have headaches all day, and they stop me from doing things," saying, "The only things I do are the things I have to do. I can't do anything for myself. If I could get rid of that headache, I feel I could do a lot of things." He notes that the headache starts when he's driving home after teaching a night class, where, he says, "Everything is good, everything is fine." The headache becomes worse as it gets closer to bedtime, which puts stress on lovemaking.

"Is there any relationship between the headache and the fantasy?"

"No, none."

"You just mentioned that you can do the 'have-to' things but not the 'want-to' things. How similar is that to the fantasy?"

"'Have-to's keep me where I'm at. But the 'want-to's? If I could do that, it would be fantastic." He adds that he is terrified when he wakes up with the headache, because he knows his whole day will be ruined. Even though the headache may last all day, it doesn't interfere with the "have-to's" but he knows it will prevent him from concentrating on what he wants. When asked to reflect on his inability to concentrate, he says, "I want to cry because I can't keep my mind on it."

He recognizes that this state of mind is familiar since childhood. I ask him to reflect on a time when it was particularly intense. He recalls an episode he'd mentioned in a previous talk.

His father had bought a lawnmower. It was a "weird" brand and it broke down soon after the purchase. Charlie described how he took it apart, saw how it worked, and identified the broken part. His dad located a parts shop some 50 miles away where they could get the needed part. They journeyed there together, got the part, and when he returned home, Charlie "put it together exquisitely," painted every part, and reflected, "It was a beautiful thing."

The lawnmower ran perfectly until the governor (the part that regulates how fast the engine will run) kicked out and the lawnmower blew up. "You don't know how to work on small things," his father had said simply.

"How did you feel when your father said that?" I ask.

Charlie says, "I think it was bullshit, but I think I believed him."

"Why? Isn't it true?"

"Is there some kind of test we can do to determine whether it's true or not?" I ask.

"I think I already passed the test [when I fixed the mower initially], but it's tough to believe it. I knew it was a poorly-designed lawnmower, but I never believed it."

He continues to work on mechanical things and feels "extremely accomplished when I can do something that's mechanical and precise." When I ask him how he understands what he's doing, he says, "I'm trying to prove him wrong."

"Would you review the lawnmower scene to see if you can prove your father wrong?"

He recollects that he took it apart, saw what was wrong, understood how the damaged part functioned, and explained it to his father. Then they drove 50 miles on his information to get new parts, and the shop owner brought *him* over to verify the part, not his father. He felt that this trip with his father was a "high" because its success depended on him alone. Then, having repaired the machine, it appeared better than it was before, since he painted each part "exquisitely" and it worked "perfectly." It started with one pull. He recognizes his father's involvement in many of the stages, but not in the final testing.

He concludes that his father was wrong.

"You both knew who was wrong," I remind him.

"When you said that," he says, "You know what hit me? I knew when we first started to try to find parts that there was a problem in the basic design of that machine. In fact, we *both* knew it was a poorly-designed machine, a 'weird' one, but we bought it because it was 'a good deal.'"

"Your father did not praise you when you had done such good work, is that right?"

"My father never gave praise, but he often ridiculed," Charlie responds. "And in fact, my father tried to take credit at the parts store. "When I first installed the part, my dad fell down laughing at it." He recalls that then, at the point he was being ridiculed, "it was the most emotion I got out of my dad." His dad left, so he didn't see Charlie fix the problem in about five minutes—and it worked perfectly after that.

"When we believe something completely contrary to the facts, there must be something important going on," I suggest.

"What the hell is going on?" says Charlie. He goes through all the evidence in his mind, but says, "I still believe it!" He pauses to think about all the projects he's done with his dad. "They all seem to have a flaw," he says.

"What kind of relationship did you have with your dad during this episode with the lawnmower?" I ask.

"It's warm and full. It's a rare thing," he says.

Exploring the sequence to the lawnmower blowing up, I ask him, "What other judgment could your father have made [at that time]?"

"It looks like he could have come out and said, "Well, I guess it's a weird machine. He had two alternatives; he could either have said 'I blew it,' or 'You blew it!'" Recognizing that he had been taking the blame, Charlie says, "If I got [the blame], that saved him."

He is reflecting on the situation. "Why would I spend my life trying to prove him wrong?" His father had known all along it was a "weird machine," but he tolerated it and within the scene, he showed himself as warm, caring father. The son also knew the machine was flawed, but revealing that would put the rare display of affection at risk.

Charlie realizes that when his father said, "You don't know how to work on small things," he had to say that rather than admit that he'd made a mistake in purchasing the flawed machine. But he quickly adds, "I wouldn't make a big deal of it; since he got it so damn cheap. Who gives a shit? We had a lot of fun." But he reflects further and realizes that if his father had admitted it was a bad purchase, he'd have to admit he'd made a mistake, and so create a new mature way of relating.

Charlie says, "That's the only way it's going to make anything worthwhile. Otherwise, that whole thing there—that's going to be love, and who the hell wants that kind of love?" Examining this lawnmower incident shows him that he thought he had had a meaningful relationship with his father. He remembers that they related "as equals," but then he exclaims, "The consequences of taking the blame—my whole being has something wrong with it," adding, "like I'm just a kid, no longer equal." He mentions, "If my father had said, 'you don't know how to work on small things' when the lawnmower was all taken apart, that would have been the obvious proof. That would have hurt worse."

Then he asks, "Why does it keep going away? It's almost as if I don't want to look at this."

"What effect does taking the blame have on your understanding about this encounter with your father?"

"It makes me forget it; it makes it a foolish thing." He adds, "My father laid the thing on me."

At this point, he makes a connection with the memory of a boat trip he had made, which is now the subject of his novel. "What keeps racing through my mind, because I found the key to the goddamn boat trip just now, and that's what's bugging me." He remembers how he had ingeniously saved a sailboat he was captaining from sinking. During a storm, the owner's son, also one of the crew, started the ship's motor, which caused the anchor chain to wrap around the propeller and caused the ship to take on water and subsequently run aground. He realizes that he also took the blame for running the ship aground: "I took it!" He realizes that by accepting that lie, he could keep the relationship with the owner's son.

Going back to the original incident, I ask, "What would have happened if you had disagreed with your father?"

"When you said that, I just felt something horrible would happen, something terrible." Seeing no other alternative, he could only "keep that pain" and "swallow that shit."

I ask again, "Why did you believe your father?" and suggest that the way to answer the question further would be to explore that state of mind in past scenes prior to the lawnmower scene, where someone in the family opposed his father.

Charlie recalls a past scene: He was a young boy riding in the back seat of the family car. The family was going to a beautiful lake site; his mother had a road map and was giving directions to his father. She told him where to turn, but he passed it. "It's not a big deal," thought Charlie, but his father insisted it was his mother's fault, saying she didn't tell him to turn in time. There was a "heavy fight between them."

Considering this scene, Charlie sees that his mother would not accept the blame in this situation and insisted it *was* his father's fault. His father put up "one hell of a fight" rather than admit to "a small error." Charlie begins to see that the blame issue was always over something trivial (because it was always clear who was wrong), so he also came to realize and accept that his parents exhibited their intense feelings through such scenes. "That's how they get it [feelings]." Thinking about the lake site, he says, "God, it was exquisite," but adds, "It wasn't a very much fantastic place after that [fight]."

Charlie reflects that these kinds of scenes "happened probably a lot of times. It's like sitting in the back seat and watching a Greek tragedy." After thinking for a while, he realizes that this is how his parents show feelings to one another, saying, "They bitch and moan at each other; that's how they communicate." He notes that they act out this drama through failures, and he notices that the failures all have a common feature: "It's the same kind of failure. It's silly."

Charlie recognizes that he uses a similar method as his parents to gain intense feelings and sense of communication. He acknowledges, "That's how it got there," or in other words, that's how he got to communicate this way to gain strong feelings.

"What does that to do beautiful places such as the lake site?" I ask.

He reflects on what he would like to have said to his father. "It's like, 'I want to save this, Dad. Let's straighten out what's going on,' but I couldn't say that; I couldn't even suggest it."

Reflecting back on the lake site trip, Charlie describes the wonder of the trip. It was the "greatest place," he says. The excitement of driving to the lake was the "peak of the trip."

I asked him to explore the relationship between the experience of excitement over the natural beauty of the lake and his father's role. He says his father's game made a profound impact on him. "It's like walking around the pine tree and seeing the ground full of shit and paper." Charlie then sees that the intensity of the fight functions to wipe out the anticipation of a beautiful experience and the state of excitement it produces.

He says that it was really the beauty of the lake he wanted to experience. I point out the outline of the talk on the blackboard. Pointing to all the goals he mentioned, he says, "It's like all these things I want to do are at the beginning of the trip. And it's almost like

I know ahead of time where they're going to go. And the more I work on them, the more confused I get."

"You have a fight within yourself?" I ask.

"It could either be a fight with myself or with my wife," he answers.

"What does that do to your goals?"

"I lose interest, because I don't want to go there."

"In the future, you could refer to your goals as 'Problems of the Lake Site,' or 'How to Make Something that is Beautiful into Something Ugly.'" He refines that by adding, "Before you get there."

"It's Dad's world!" he says. "God! He's inviting me to have a love affair with him," but then rephrases it, "Enter Dad's world." He explains. "He's asking me to throw away all that. I wouldn't do it."

I suggest, "You may want to examine all your present events where your goals are similar to the lake site scene. We'll see what happens when you try to go for them. Now, let's review all that we did in this session."

Going over the list of things he wanted to discuss, Charlie comments, "There are certain fights here [on the list] and that fits that."

Barbara

[Note: This dialogue, along with the drawings, come from *The Way of the Logos, Volume 1, The Demonstration*, 2011, by Pierre Grimes. These drawings are typical of the kind of drawings done during PM sessions.]

This dialogue took place at a seminar where there were others present.

Barbara: I'm having a problem remembering things that I already know. Like this morning, Pierre asked me what a Greek word means, *skolia*, and I had no idea. I felt passive and stupid, but when I heard someone else say what it meant—I thought, I know that! But at the time it didn't seem worthwhile to figure it out.

Pierre: But you already knew the answer?

Barbara: Yes, with a certain amount of effort. Really I was blocked and couldn't get past it, a problem I often have with my Greek studies so I always find myself going to the lexicon even though I know the words.

Pierre: What does it do to you? You know how to answer that?

Barbara: No. Well, yes and no.

Pierre: I'll take the yes.

Barbara: I feel like I just locked a further door of a prison cell, rather than unlocking it.

Pierre: A jail within a jail? Would you mind describing yourself in the jail?

Barbara: Well, I'm all bent over. And my arms are…energy-less; they just hang. I'm real, real stuck. I feel really scummy like I'm in a sludge.

Pierre: Oh yes, I'm familiar with that word. I had a friend who used to work with one.

Barbara: Oh! A sludge hammer! [laughter]

Pierre: Do you notice that we have a little fun, talking like this? There's a freedom in it, isn't there? Now watch what happens when we go back into the problem.

Barbara: Oh, I'm not in the jail when we're joking.

Pierre: Now let's go back into the jail. You said a moment ago that you didn't think it was worthwhile to pursue the answer, right?

Barbara: Yes, because whether I got it right or not, I'd be in isolation, jail.

Pierre: Because?

Barbara: Because somehow if I get the Greek word and I feel really good about it and I show it, the result is the same as if I couldn't find the word and didn't understand.

Pierre: Could you go over that again?

Barbara: Hmmm. It looks like I'm looking for a transformation of some kind. What I want would be happiness, like people would say, "Oh yes, that's right," and there would be unity. But that's not going to happen. So whatever I do, it doesn't matter.

Pierre: So instead of unity, isolation follows. Let's go back and look again. Julie, why don't you be an actress and Barbara will be the director and she will tell you what to do, to act out her part in this problem. Julie, you be the one trying to remember a Greek word, and Barbara will tell you how to act as you do it.

Barbara: OK, first you have to be considering it, and then you have to get it, and you have to be really excited about it.

Julie: OK [and does it], "Oh, yeah."

Barbara: No, no, you can't whisper it; you have to shout it, and then you have to jump up and say, "I got it!"

Julie, Oh, yeah! [jumps up] I got it! Eureka! That's it!

Pierre: Now tell the group what their part should be in this drama.

Barbara: Well, you people should be all pissed off. You're looking down and won't see what Julie's doing at all.

Pierre: Then what happens?

Barbara: She goes, "Oh, you're right," and sits down.

Pierre: OK. Let's do it. Go ahead.

Julie: [shouting] I got it!

Audience: Boo! It's shitty, boo!

Pierre: But she did get it. The audience doesn't know that, but if she agrees with those people, is she agreeing with those who know or those who don't know?

Barbara: They don't know, but she gave up. She could have walked out.

Pierre: But you chose not to. You have to give up what you know and agree with what is not true. When she agrees with their judgment and sits down, how is that like the sludge?

Barbara: It's the same; it's the sludgy state. I'm trying to find some way of attacking that sludge but.... [pauses, struggles] it's like I'm wrestling with it, but it's so heavy and I get weaker and just stop. I try to get out and that's the struggle.

Pierre: What's it like when you are trying to get out?

Barbara: Oh, like I don't have any idea of what would work. I don't have any notion of how to get out. It has no form, no point of attack. It's all the same, there's no difference in it, nothing I can choose. I'm just stuck with it.

Pierre: What does it take to get out of that sludge? Do you see yourself struggling?

Barbara: The image is like—like it's my mother. It's like going to the lexicon. It requires a kind of endurance, a slow-moving strength, like an elephant pushing something, but a stupid, kind of like a blind-pushing quality.

Pierre: That is a fine description but there's one part I didn't get: "It's like my mother." There are many scenes you could choose from your life with her.

Barbara: But she's in that state frequently, a lot. I can see her in the front room. I'm thirteen. And she's doing something, cooking or baking. My father is there; he's talking.

Barbara: Father is there. And my father is talking, and that is unusual for him. He doesn't talk a lot. Whatever he's saying is really bugging my mother and she pretends that she doesn't hear him and goes on with what she's doing. She has that sense of steeling, what we say in my family, "steeling yourself up." It's like putting on armor.

Pierre: Then he's silent? But he's "bugging her"? Go ahead, just tell the story.

Barbara: Well, she just goes on with what she's doing—for a long time. He keeps bugging her. This is building up feelings in her and I get the feeling that she wants to smother someone.

Pierre: What do you mean?

Barbara: She wants to—she'd like to—if she could just—she'd like to put some kind of a blanket over it that would, that would—

Pierre: Over what?

Barbara: My father. And over what he was doing in the house so he would be quiet and wouldn't move and it's like she wants to—just deaden it, stop it right there, immobilize it.

Barbara: What's unique about my father is that when he bursts into a conversation, it's with a great deal of energy. And so he continues with that. He'll do it, and jump in again, again, and again, and it builds up. It's almost as if he's not watching her, as though he is not watching her, but the effect builds.

27

Pierre: He's blind to it?

Barbara: Well, he gives that appearance of not paying any attention. I'm not sure if that's true, but that's what it looks

Pierre: You're watching it? Anyone else around at the time?

Barbara: I don't know if anybody else was watching it. It seems like nobody else was there. But I'm walking in and walking out, walking in, walking out. I'm getting extremely anxious and my stomach is getting all tied up in knots. So my mother tries to pull me in on it in some way. She makes some comment to me, on the side, kind of an aside that I'm supposed to jump in on her side and put my father down.

Pierre: Right, it's a message, and therefore you know what you should do?

Barbara: Yes, but I feel—I really—I feel a lot of conflict about doing that, because I don't want to see him—I don't want to help in that. But she keeps pressing; she keeps pushing at me about it.

Barbara: And then I get the feeling from her that I'm going to get chopped up into little pieces if I don't do it. So I try to find a way to say something that isn't one or the other. It's a failure. It doesn't succeed either way. She's pissed at me and he's pissed at me. And he's depressed because he thinks I joined her camp. I tried to do both but I failed and it ended up working against me in both ways, but I didn't get destroyed by my mom.

Pierre: Which is pretty good. So then, what's happening? How would your dad see you? Give me a name, please.

Barbara: He would see me as a betrayer, but that's not really the word I'm thinking of. He'd see me as— well, as a woman, as a fink.

Pierre: And your mother? How does she see you?

Barbara: As fighting her will. She's getting something but she's not getting everything she wants—about ten percent. But my father doesn't seem to see that that's all she's getting. He sees it like a total concession. That stops things for a while; it stops the build-up.

Barbara: He's pissed off. And let's see: it seems like there was a certain release from her. They seem to end

74

up kind of together, but I go off feeling—[struggling for words]—well, they end up talking about me in one sense, but you know, they are kind of conferring, so they are close. And I end up looking like a retarded, crippled individual, slumping off into the sunset.

I'm terrible all my fault ⑦

Pierre: Talk about their view of you at this point.

Barbara: It's like I need their help, but I'm—stubborn. They are saying I need them—because they are saying, "She never grew up and she's not going to grow up." I'm crying. They predict I'll never grow up; they're prophets, that I won't succeed, like I said earlier about the Greek. When I leave the room, they are very sweet, but I feel all foggy. I fog it out. But they look really clear and happy together, tranquil, delighted.

Alternative:
What would happen
if I didn't save them?

Scene

① Barbara 8 yr. — Brother sister all watching and listening

② tension builds up! "The Review of Sins"

Father: No Love, no sex
No talking
You don't care!
all past sins - personal!

Mother: I clean the house for you - ...Cinderella...

③ "... they both have some good.."
pain anguish
proof of Love: SACRIFICE

④ Divorce!
we will be destitute
we will be on the street

a Split!

Pierre: Do you understand this?

Barbara: No, I don't understand it.

Pierre: Then memory isn't enough. What don't you understand?

76

Barbara: Well, it jumped into my mind that I don't understand why I was in this scene with them.

Pierre: If you hadn't been in this scene, what would have happened?

Barbara: They would have a big fight. They would start going over their whole existence together, and they'd be picking out all the major crimes they could attribute to one another. Each one tops the other; they dredge up everything, in front of me.

Pierre: So they are letting you see something, aren't they?

Barbara: Yes, what they think of each other. And this sort of—purifies them. They end up feeling really good about themselves and each sees the other as the cause of their entire problem.
Barbara: I was seeing that she regards the sacrifice as proof that she cares for him. Both seem to think that what the other one wants is bad. He says that what she calls love is not love. Then he gets mad.

Pierre: You can't screw a grouch?

Barbara: True. That is what he says about it!

Pierre: Put it in your own words.

Barbara: It's not enough, what she wants. [She struggles for words.] I think he'd say, "Housework is not caring for someone." Then the kids come into the scene. They are silent, and the kids go to each of them, and they look like parents again, and everything is all right. I was worrying that the family would break up, that we'd be on the streets, but I went in and tried to bring everything back together again. I become the problem, so they can be the lovers who are going to help me out.

Pierre: What name would you give to describe your role in all this?

Barbara: Scapegoat.

Pierre: You do bring them together, don't you? And what role is that?

Barbara: Pimp.

Pierre: Pimp? So you act for another, save them from putting into words what they most desire? Is there an honorific title for your function?

Barbara: Cupid? Ah-ha! Eros?

Miguel [speaking for the first time]: It's one of the roles of the midwife, isn't it, matchmaker?

Pierre: So your role in the house is a very important role, Cupid, matchmaker, Eros. Do they need a Cupid or an Eros?

Barbara: Yes, well, I believed they did. It seems like it involves a whole world view at one extreme, like a story that's been told that has this need that they stay together, because if they were to come apart, it would be horrible for the family. Mother would be by herself; she couldn't support the family; we'd be on the street, in rags; we'd starve to death.

Pierre: Then it's more than Cupid and Eros—you are saving...

Barbara: The family, like a hero, so there's a fog but there's kind of a nobility about the fog, like it's absent-minded, like there's no...memory of what went on before.

Pierre: Because?

Barbara.: Well, if I were to remember it, I'd be pissed off because those two were the cause of it but I got left with it.

Pierre: So you have to be the forgetful one, and there is a nobility in forgetting, so take this forgetting and that nobility, and give it a name.

Barbara: It's like...a priest in the confessional. I'm forgiving their sins!

Pierre: And the officiating priest forgets it all? But what does it mean when you forgive and forget their sins?

Barbara: It means it never happened. And you have to keep it secret, because there's nobility in that too. And the secret is—that I'm not retarded and not—forgetful.

Pierre: You mean you're not the image they have of you and want you to be?

Barbara: No! I'm not.

Pierre: Then the fog prevents you from seeing them, but it also prevents you from seeing yourself.

Barbara: So I have to accept that image of myself as a retarded person, to keep the family together. We all forget about the whole thing, till the next time. I feel I have to be very serious about it, when I'm in it.

Pierre: You can't tell a joke in the middle of these things, can you?

Barbara: Or when they're in the middle of it, you can't say, "Well, guys, if I don't help you out here, you're going to break up, huh? Now is that what you really want me to believe? But you know you never do it. So why do you play out this lousy game?" I could never say that.

Pierre: And they often talked you over? What kinds of things did they say about you?

Barbara: Well, they were loving, but they love me retarded, baby-like.

Pierre: So there will be some value in staying that way and never growing up. So this secret game becomes love. That's your role in the loving game, is that right? And how do they look when they are talking to you?

Barbara: Warm, cheerful, relaxed, but that's the only time they ever seem that way. They are together, and they are at the top, like on a mountain, a peak, that's their "high." They look...like gods, fine, and beautiful—and right.

Pierre: And you are helping them achieve this "high?" You've never seen them so high, so beautiful, so right? That's quite an ideal scene to participate in! You see them in their noblest and finest moments, so you cannot fail to be impressed. In such scenes, we "learn" something. By the way, did your sister go through this when she was 13 too?

Barbara: Hard to tell, but I think so.

Pierre: What's the significance of that, going through it when you're 13?

Barbara: Well, we girls do develop at that time, puberty. But I was dressed in a shapeless outfit, kind of retarded. If I looked like I was growing up, then the relationships would change. Otherwise, my mother couldn't be on the mountaintop because there would be other peaks showing. [Laughter] But my mother

82

won't see anything my father does as any good. She wants to flatten him out. And she uses this tone of voice, a very magnificent, full tone of voice, "Oh, your father was always like this." She's trying to show no emotion, no irritation. She's pretending she's never irritated by him. And she looks very wise, warm, witty, knowing.

Pierre: So what are you seeing in this great scene?

Barbara: That that is what knowing is! That's how you show your knowing.

Pierre: So you see how to use knowledge, when to use it, and how to show when you have it. So what does it do, this knowing? This wisdom?

Barbara: Well, when someone really wants to talk, and—they're feeling energy but also agony or pain— that's the time you become increasingly aloof—when he's trying to show himself. And seeing that puts you in a state of knowing so you don't talk to that person or interact with him at all. You cut him off, so he becomes—powerless.

Pierre: How often did you see your dad wanting to talk with that much energy, anguish, pain, and yet cut off?

Barbara: Not that often. But at that time, he really wanted to talk to her, to relate to her, he's sincere, but she smothers it, so he's—powerless.

Pierre: So you learned what the conditions of sincerity are, where sincerity goes, and how it is blocked, how it can be channeled, how it can be robbed, how it can be stripped, how to deal with a man who is being sincere, who wants to talk.

Barbara: Yes, and he was not often like that.

Pierre: When they were talking to each other, did they speak clearly?

Barbara: No, they kept rephrasing everything each time.

Pierre: You have to hide, disguise, change what you mean? So while you're communicating, you're stumbling around, changing things?

Barbara: Yes! So in my role, you also have to do that, or you'll be taking sides. You have to be really careful of what you're doing and how you say it so it doesn't go one way or the other. It has to put me right in the middle, and I have to look like a dope. I feel afraid that I'm going to screw up.

Pierre: What would happen if you didn't side with your mother?

Barbara: She would tear me apart piece by piece. I had to. Like, she would choose all my things—the things most dear to me—and she cut them up. Like I would go out on nature walks and bring things back, things of beauty that I collected, but she didn't consider them beautiful...

Pierre: So you introduced a new idea of beauty into the house? A competing idea of beauty?

Barbara: Yes, more related to my father than to her, because he spent his spare time out in the country, nature walks, too, but she'd talk about my collections as if she were revealing my crimes. She'd take up one of my things, that she knew was valuable to me, and talk about it as if it were really evil. I was convinced by it. She'd talk about my dad the same way, and I'd say, "There's not a problem with what he's doing. It's OK; it's fine to do." Then she would annihilate me for saying that. I felt that if I didn't do what she said or agree with her, that she'd do the same thing to me, wipe out all the things I thought were beautiful, everything I loved.

Pierre: Tell me: Did your mom have anything to do with church?

Barbara: Yes, she's from the Church of God.

Pierre: What's her favorite theological expression? Let's guess: "Thou...."

Barbara: "Thou shalt have no other gods before me." Yes! She has her own pulpit and if you don't pay allegiance to that, watch out!

Pierre: Behind that, there are many theological themes. How about, "Thou shalt not find beauty anywhere else"?

Barbara: But she was beautiful when she was in the problem-game. But to see it, I had to act retarded. So...I'm supposed to find something beautiful only by being retarded...

Pierre: Well, sometimes these things do take sacrifices, like you have to perish for her sins?

Barbara: The Christ figure! So that's why I end up feeling so noble when I wipe myself out. All that suffering—the depth of it just makes you feel good about yourself. I am getting this!

Pierre: So how many philosophical concepts do you see in this? Did you learn about what's noble, good, beautiful? And what is knowledge, wisdom, sincerity, and how to handle these ideas? And love? Sacrifice? How to fight?

Barbara: Yes. And I only remember enough to go through this the next time.

Pierre: So we have to explore the nature of the devices that keep us from seeing, which is to erect blocks or obstacles to prevent or limit seeing it, discussing it, and understanding it. The blocks seem so formidable, so impregnable, but in reality it's only a paper tiger that scares us away from seeing what we need to know. Yet to a child it seems so frightening that it works. Why could we not have said, "Let's talk about this, Mom and Dad?"

Barbara: That would have been impossible.

Pierre: Then it's fair to say that it would upset the whole family structure if you could have talked about it?

Barbara: Oh, yes!

Pierre: In other words, there must be a formidable defense. It must be an anti-speculation, anti-intellectual, anti-reflective attitude, or else it could be challenged. And that is what prevents us from being able to see.

Contents and Elements of the Pathologos

Reading these talks can help us understand how our mental life is an interconnected web of beliefs or thoughts. When we feel discomfort or disharmony, it's because this web has been upset or muddled with ideas that are inconsistent and contrary with the beliefs we have. *How* uncomfortable we encounter that we feel depends on how much the beliefs are distorted—and our life reflects that in confusion and suffering.

These distorted ideas are the *content* of the pathologos. They layer the family's unhealthy, personal interpretations and meanings over our own thoughts, creating two frames of reference and two levels of communication: one, where we can *see* meanings but don't believe they apply to us; and two, where we incorrectly interpret things in our life—and then accept it as the absolute truth.

We build up these personal interpretations from early experiences drawn together in a system of ideas like a vortex, sweeping everything significant into the private and narrow language of the family or clan. Philosophical Midwifery (PM) provides a system of questions and answers (which we can also call *the dialectic)*, which brings this hidden network of belief into the light of reason, and traces back each of the themes of the pathologos until we see the root belief of the pathologos, revealing the defenses that bind the family into a unity, giving its members both role models and a complete system of ideas for relating to the world.

Still, whether or not a pathologos is present, the family depends on every member participating in a system of ideas which make up the truth about themselves and their reality. This system of ideas gives the family unity; it gives them an identity, a place, and a sense of belonging and harmony. When they no longer participate in that unity, they will scatter and no longer have that family identification— an identification they used to feel was essential.

Beliefs

So we can see that *beliefs* — whether true or false — bind us together as families. And we can trace our false beliefs back to a particular, fundamental belief, the pathologos. The influence of all these beliefs — and especially the pathologos — on our life is extraordinary.

The pathologos sets up the conditions for the degeneration of religious beliefs into the false beliefs of the family, so the family problems become the family religion — or cult. The pathologos functions like a commandment, spreading throughout the family life, but it is not preached beyond the family because it only works within the context of the family. Everyone in the family learns it and believes it, but nobody ever discusses it. No one ever challenges it, either; that would be presumptuous. So each member accepts it as something basic about who they are — and about what is real!

In this way, the family imposes a system of ideas on all its members, a system of ideas that becomes the way the family thinks and reasons. It is fundamentally destructive, because it weakens our ability to plan, care for, and reflect on our lives. Thus we can think of it as a psychic parasite, because it robs its host of a healthy life, psychologically and even physically.

Think about the talk with Anna. The primary expression of her pathologos was this: that understanding was a gift only to be given to the worthy, so if she *did* understand something, it would create a conflict among those who believe they *aren't* worthy of it. She felt unworthy, so she could never understand things. Now think of Charlie. The primary expression of his pathologos was a world-denying idea typical of those who have to deny what is good and beautiful, because they fear the wrath of their jealous God who cannot tolerate believers loving anyone than himself.

Even though the families of Anna and Charlie did not express the pathologos in religious terms, these are religious beliefs—only in this case, the parents become like God: hostile to all who compete for their children's affection and love, demanding that their children relate exclusively to them, causing the children to sacrifice their own goals for the parents and to work only for the goals of the parents. In such cases, they undermine and devalue their children's efforts to achieve the ideal. Playing out the role of God, or priest, or minister, on the family is the root of many problems. In families where religion does play an active role, it's not unusual to find the family acting out the Garden of Eden tale, punishing their young children and exiling them when in moments of openness and innocence. These family expressions are different from adult experiences of theology and religion, which have their place—which is not being played out on the unsuspecting members of one's own family.

When we separate from our pathologos, our false belief, we go into crisis. Some people can't bear it and withdraw from the process of PM, either completely or for various periods of time. The most difficult thing about it is losing those intense, high states of mind which provide people a role, or way of being, which they believed to be essential to them. Separating from the pathologos removes the model of a familiar, predictable world and takes us into a strange, new, and open world.

Perhaps the hardest thing is giving up the *knower* role, where we appear powerful and important, where we feel a particular intensity not usually present in the non-pathologos experience. Most people admire and love that powerful role, so when we realize it's part of a false belief, we often feel deeply disillusioned. Of course, we all want to get rid of the pain of the pathologos, but when we discover that the high goes with the low—inseparably—it's a real shock. Faced with giving up that high, purging themselves of the high intense state, some would rather discontinue the talks or adjust their lives rather than give it up. They would rather be a "king among lesser men" and keep their appearance of power than give it up for being an equal among equals.

Clinging to that high prevents us from pursuing our higher goals, but people sometimes would rather give them up, pursuing secondary goals and absorbing themselves in practical pursuits, like those in Goethe's *Faust*, who think their epic excavation project is to reclaim land, when it is only to dig Faust's grave. Giving up that high, intense state sometimes seems too steep a price to pay for our own maturity. Some people cannot bear to give up their idealized image of the parents, so they cling to the illusion.

However, when people are willing to give up the false belief, the illusion, without being angered by what they have learned, their new view of things will not let them blame their parents. They are now free to experience the world fresh and "unknowing," liberated from their old models.

It's clear enough that most of us will benefit from Philosophical Midwifery, but there is something that will probably drive us to do it. It is this: remaining in our pathologos problems makes us feel profoundly alienated and immobilized by futility. Most of us loathe these feelings so much that we would do just about anything to get out of them. We go to war, use drugs, get married or even play golf.

These feelings may drive us into psychotherapy, quests for heavenly intervention, Zen meditation, into the priesthood or into coaching Little League. It may be the reason we sell our talents and life's energy to enrich a corporation with the vague promise of financial gain and possibly retirement.

Seems like we'll try anything, except for one thing, which is the one thing which will release us: relying on our own reason to resolve our conflicts and our dissatisfaction with life. Most of us think that feelings determine our lives, but the reality is that we live our lives through our *minds*.

We resolve our conflicts only through our minds, and we eventually understand the unity of life through our minds. This helps us resolve our feelings, and eventually leads us to a deeper understanding of the mystery of our existence. The way to this understanding is the ancient path of philosophy.

True: most of us think of philosophy as a pointless, dry intellectual exercise (that's what our college courses gave us). Worse, many of us think of philosophy as hostile—or at least indifferent—to spirituality and metaphysics. Philosophy in the university tradition (which is in the European tradition) attempts to find meaning in history, language, science, even common sense, but not to "know thyself." Most professors and students at universities would consider studying philosophy as a quest for wisdom to be not only unscientific but irrelevant—if not heretical.

In fact, in our modern times, many of us feel skeptical about reason; we distrust it. But this is not the fault of reason itself. The problem is that we have ignored our past, not rejected it. Our culture has turned its back on the profound traditions of our past. Thus, the claim that philosophy can give us meaning and explain the workings of our minds is something most people would consider ridiculous. Sadly, many of us who have turned to the most profound Eastern philosophies have found they don't engage reason or the intellect, either.

The ancient Greeks, in contrast with the European tradition we've all grown up with in high school and college, cultivated philosophy as a quest for wisdom, which helped them to achieve profound spiritual goals. Philosophical Midwifery adapts this ancient method to reveal something we never suspected (though we know it from our daily experience): we are in the grip of some strange kind of problem.

We know that any false belief about ourselves or about reality blocks us from reaching our highest aspirations and most meaningful goals. We also know that our false beliefs are invisible to us. Since we don't even know we believe these false beliefs, we can't even think about them! We accept them as absolutely true; our intuition backs us up on this, but we can't even articulate what they are. Thus we are trapped in the worst kind of ignorance. We believe we are intelligent and good enough, but at the same time, we have no idea how we ended up so far from our ideals and goals. We can't see why we fall into our all-too-familiar destructive patterns, especially right when we're ready to succeed. We desperately need to understand ourselves, to understand reality, but we have no way to address our predicament.

Well, how could philosophy help us out of this deep problem?

The practice of philosophy starts with ignorance—or not knowing—and uses a careful method of reasoning to right opinion, to understanding, to knowledge and to wisdom. It moves, like a flight of stairs, from ignorance to wisdom.

Why even take this journey? It's because when we remain ignorant of our false beliefs, we block our development—totally, irrevocably. We will continue to fail in life, to feel disillusioned. Sure, we can "learn" the right opinions or the right answers, but it won't help us much unless we understand the reasons for the answer being right.

How can reason reveal incorrect beliefs you never knew you had? Reason functions in philosophy the same way it does in the sciences. Follow the steps of reason and you will arrive at the right answers, just the same as you follow the steps of scientific reason to come to a reliable answer.

We can observe patterns in our life, in our behavior, in our dreams, even in the subatomic world of quarks and superstrings. When we search for the causes of patterns in the heavens, it's called cosmology; when we search for the causes of our believing false beliefs, into the processes of reaching understanding, into the nature of our mind, it is called philosophy.

It stands to reason that there must be a way out of the false beliefs that hold us back and keep us unhappy. There has to be a way to find the false beliefs that lie beneath our problems. True, every problem is unique, but since the general form of all problems is pretty much the same, so there needs to be a set of questions we can use to address them.

Philosophical Midwifery gives us that set of questions. I've used this method for many years to introduce people to self-reflection and help deliver them from their false beliefs. These questions will bring to the surface the nature of your problems.

The Beliefs, The Milieu, and Pathologos Themes

Here are the main elements of the pathologos, which connect together in a network of ideas: the core beliefs, the milieu, and the pathologos themes.

The *core beliefs* of the pathologos are the false beliefs about your self and about reality. These beliefs seem to circle around the axis of your self, like a cylinder, which creates the sense of stability and support of this false image of your self. Of course, the sense of stability is really just an illusion, which gets more and more distorted as it moves away from the center—you.

These core beliefs of the pathologos dominate us with a force and presence that block everything but their own message. They make up different aspects of the pathologos and are charged with feeling, since they include blaming yourself and others, and doubting yourself and your ability to understand. They seem to be true, to exist as truths about your self. They seem to be rational, so we never suspect how irrational they are.

The *milieu* is the repeated patterns of family relationships that make up the family's usual background of events, and it is also the context within which the pathologos shows up. Family members accept it as normal, but this "normality" always contains key elements of the pathologos. Even though the pathologos is accepted as true and rational, the pathologos scene is always highly charged emotionally, and it seems to have the mark of truth, since it stresses the supposed "truth" of the milieu.

While there are disturbing and puzzling contradictions within the milieu, the family never resolves them, but always tolerates them. To outsiders, there doesn't seem to be anything particularly wrong with the milieu, but for the members of the family, it constantly reminds them of the pathologos, so it is the vehicle for it. Understanding the pathologos will allow us to understand the milieu—and to defeat it.

You can't have a pathologos without the milieu, because some of the key elements of the pathologos act as symbols for its power. Unless you challenge those key elements of the pathologos, it stays in place. As symbols, they trigger or cue the drama of the pathologos, giving the milieu a kind of stamp of finality and respectability. These symbols are strong and enduring, and hold the pathologos in place. They hover around the family, a constant reminder of the power of the pathologos. They create a constant pressure in which the family tries to survive.

These symbols return as thoughts and images that harass you and produce tension and states of mind that block your progress. The persistence of these symbols is a sign that the parental image is still intact, that you are loyal to it. They are a defense against seeing and naming what has been going on. Our reluctance to properly name the way a central figure in the pathologos (usually a parent) has been functioning keeps the symbols in place. Of course, it's good to be loyal to one's family, but loyalty that keeps a destructive family pathologos in place can never be good. When a person matures and grows out of the web of the pathologos, some families launch a counter-attack to keep the person inside the web, insisting on the appropriate response to the symbols of the milieu, because the milieu and pathologos have created a boundary within which the family/clan limits personal growth and development.

People who have broken through the power of the pathologos often find they must struggle against these symbols when they go home or deal with family members. Even telephone calls or letters contain these symbols, causing you a struggle so long as some residue of belief in still in place. Staying loyal to the pathologos means staying with fixed patterns of behavior, since people generally stick with what they think has worked in the past.

Family members recognize the behaviors as part of their family patterns—which are formed by the pathologos drama. These patterns can show up through grandparents, parents, and their children. Outsiders may find much of this incomprehensible, but once you can interpret the pathologos, grasping the meaning of the symbols, you can make sense of the puzzling patterns and repetitions of the milieu.

Some elements of the pathologos are more public expressions of it and are the tolerated, less obnoxious elements of it. The milieu functions to make it seem acceptable and somewhat normal for discordant elements to exist alongside normal behavior of the family. Tolerating these elements actually supports the entire pathologos, including its more bizarre and harmful aspects. Imagine the milieu as a cloud hovering around the pathologos, like a torus figure — a 3-D circular figure — wrapped around a cylinder.

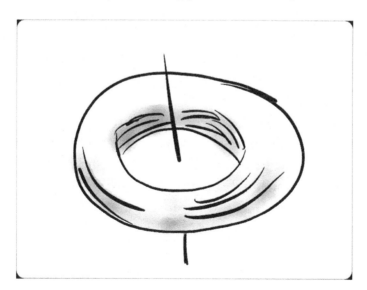

Think about the milieu with Anna, in the repetition of the sham tutoring sessions with her father. The situation might seem normal: a father helps his daughter with math. Yet think about the struggle within the milieu: she knew her role as well as her father's. She knew she could not *show* she understood the math. She also knew her father couldn't help her with math. She either had to tolerate this repeated drama or question it, but if she were to end the drama, she would also put an end to the primary way her father related to her. She couldn't challenge the drama without forcing her parents to face the fact that these unhealthy tutoring sessions had been going on for years, most every Sunday night.

The mother was an accountant and urged her daughter to let her father help her with her math homework. If she had learned her math at school she would have ended her relationship with her father and stifle her mother's desire for her to do this game.

She did not challenge the milieu and so left those scenes convinced she couldn't learn mathematics like other people. She was sure her very nature was flawed, so it was best for her to bluff and avoid being caught by those who really knew. The ideas that she is flawed, and that she cannot understand, are the core beliefs of herself and her reality.

We can see these *pathologos themes* in her inner reflections about her family. She said that her parents couldn't understand, either. If they could get by without having to demonstrate their understanding of such things, then so could she. She should not be expected to go beyond what they did: to bluff instead of to learn, and to try to avoid being found out. Accepting these things to be true, she gained a feeling of belonging, of being a member of the family. The pathologos themes support the core belief, and they support the milieu.

Of course, it's not that the parents didn't or couldn't understand math (her father was a college graduate and a flight instructor in the service). A simple review of the material would have prepared him to help her. But he chose to bluff his way through, and so continued a pattern that was consistent with other aspects of the family. He was certainly *able* to help her, but he couldn't or wouldn't find a way to explain fourth- to eighth-grade math to his daughter.

The conclusions we make about those past scenes continue in the present as thoughts and images about our self. They repeat their messages, they have a tone of urgency about them, and they seem compelling and convincing. They keep reminding us, "This is your reality." The message keeps pounding away, sometimes as a shout, and sometimes as a whisper, so that we continue to be pummeled with the original conflict and tension.

We hold onto these conclusions because without them, we would be at a loss to know when we are loved or accepted.

We would be unable to appear as knowers before others. Even arguing with ourselves about the conclusions tends to hold them in place, producing insecurity and turmoil which actually reinforce the pathologos. We argue with it, of course, because we have an inner sense that the infliction of the belief was unjust, that the belief violates our intuitive understanding of the world. Yet we bump up against the pathologos time and time again when it short-circuits our goals. The pathologos will remain in force as long as we do not overcome it—and it resists our efforts! If our struggle with it stops, it's either because the false belief has dissipated, or that the belief has overtaken us with little or no opposition, that is, as a psychosis.

The *pathologos themes* are linked together in a network of distorted reflections which support and maintain the pathologos. These themes contain the elements of past archetypal learning scenes, reflections on the milieu, and problems in the present. Each of the themes belongs to a category, or set of ideas, which influence how we function and express a particular problem as it connects with other levels. By themselves, the themes seem like parts of a puzzle that confound us, till we understand their place in a category (or set of ideas).

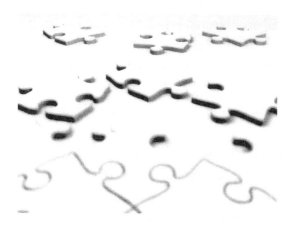

The dialectic proceeds like this: uncovering pathologos themes, tracing their connections, and bringing the whole into a unity so that we can see the underlying pathologos. This work uncovers the semantic confusion among the themes (or in other words, confusion about words and phrases), so that the more significant themes—and their relationships to one another—become clearer till the root pathologos becomes obvious. We may never understand the root pathologos unless we first bring to light and understand these themes.

Think about Charlie and the drama of the lawnmower to see how the milieu and the beliefs interplay. It seemed to Charlie that he had a rare but warm and equal relationship with his father when he did his best to fix the lawnmower. However, when the project failed, the father blamed the son and called him incompetent rather than admitting his own role in the failure. He reverted to his old role of ridiculing his son. If Charlie had challenged his father's judgment, rejecting it as false, he would have to admit that his relationship with his father was flawed by his father's pattern of ridicule—the milieu. Preserving his positive image of the father/son relationship had a cost: he had to live with his father's view that he was incapable of judging not only his own work but also the relationship he had with his father. If each project had a basic flaw, then he maintained a relationship with the work structurally similar to what he had with his father. Thus, the theme of incompetence runs through everything, and it is impossible to achieve anything but the most practical and mundane goals.

Charlie's experience with his father's ridicule left him feeling unworthy. Of course, we might suggest he could ask his father why he repeatedly ridicules, or why his mother tolerates it. But that would threaten the basic way the father relates to the son, which the son recalls as being so positive. This is the milieu. The father-inventor could not admit that his son could work on small machines without making an exception to his pattern of ridicule.

Remembering the critical past event, and understanding the meaning of what both father and son were doing, would make it possible to totally remember the whole event. We know that *amnesia* is an essential aspect of every pathologos. Our pathologos dominates us to the degree to which we have forgotten important past scenes, remembering only the *conclusions*, which become the elements of the pathologos. We can overcome the amnesia; we can remember what really happened, when we uncover the pathologos. Then we can challenge the pathologos and all that it influences, including our image of ourselves, our role, gestures, and attitudes that we formerly felt essential and basic to ourselves.

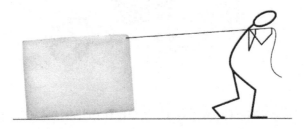

Anna, then, will need to explore the beginnings and meanings of her belief that she is unworthy, because behind each judgment or conclusion she makes about her unworthiness, there is a past scene that she needs to recall and review. Until she remembers enough, she may learn statistics (a secondary goal), but may not continue on to achieve her deepest and most meaningful goals.

Anna's solution—"get by without mastery"—only perpetuates her problem. She wants to be like her parents as well as to conform to her mother's perception of her, but she also wants to master her studies. The solution of bluffing postpones the task of

110

understanding into the indefinite future, so the problem will continue.

Charlie knew that he had repaired the lawnmower perfectly, yet after it blew up, he accepted the blame, even though both he and his father knew that the lawnmower was poorly designed and would eventually blow up in just the way it did. However, if he believed his father, he would have to conclude that he, the son, was incapable of judging (even though he brought the project to perfection) and would also be forced to conclude that his father knew all along that he was incompetent and was just pretending to have a helping and sharing relationship. Charlie had to prove his father wrong without provoking him or making him mad; thus he had to achieve without success. His solution was to complete all his projects while ignoring the fact that he too tolerated design flaws in each one. He could then appear to himself to reject his father's judgment while actually confirming it, thus preserving the image/myth of his relationship with his father as unique, that is, one in which they showed their best to one another.

We can see that we try to solve the problem of the pathologos with a *compromise* that contains the elements of the past scenes, lived repeatedly in the present. Accepting this compromise becomes a key part of the milieu and sets up a model for similar compromises in the future—or for surrender. As long as we don't understand the scenes, they have a compelling force that binds the believers into a unity, now and in the future, but once we understand the pathologos, we can separate ourselves from it, as if from shackles.

The pathologos has a compelling urgency and finality to it because, while the content is false, it serves a fundamental—though temporary—need. When we see the compromise, when we accept it, it shows us that we have embraced the milieu. The compromise made us accept a role which defines our relationships in the family and with ourselves. When we are under the influence of the pathologos, it seems so natural and intuitively certain to conclude as we did, for it provided a way to relate to our reality.

The *compromise* became the model through which we anticipate and understand our life. Just as those who were present with us during the compromise scenes seemed so convincing and sincere, so in our later lives, we too take on a similar appearance and function. From scenes that appear similar, we continue to act in a similar way. The pathologos has affected us so deeply that we cannot appreciate differences between then and now. We enter into a waking dream, acting out a pathologos drama as we once saw it play out before us.

In these situations, we imitate those roles and match the sincerity and confidence that influenced us, although it actually lacks any real meaning. But in acting out these roles, we expect others to be influenced and as moved as we were before. When it works out this way, we are intuitively drawn into a world that seems so familiar.

We act out the scene and influence others the way we were influenced. The compromise becomes an ideal to imitate, and the roles become acceptable within the milieu. The role we play out is a concrete expression and a manifestation of our core beliefs about our self. The pathologos restructures everything in terms of itself, and determines what's significant and what isn't. This requires that we forget what really happened; it produces the amnesia, removing the value of all that came before it.

The feelings are so strong in the compromise scene: masks of sincerity, confidence, knowing, strength, truthfulness, and beauty. These are imitation virtues, but the experience is powerful—enough to maintain a loyalty and group identity. It is clear, though, that these fake virtues can never provide for real growth and development of the mind. Even so, when we consider the effect on us of the false virtues within the pathologos, we can also see how being genuine and possessing true virtues will have a powerful effect on ourselves and on others.

The Dialectic
Asking Questions, Guiding the Dialogue...

It may seem hard to believe, but every pathologos has the same structure, function and goal. Because these show up every time, we often speak of the form of the pathologos problem—which you could also call its *morphology*.

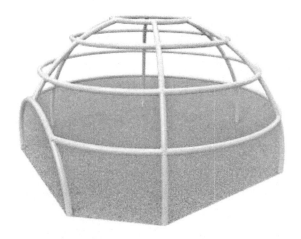

Over the years, I've discovered a set of questions, and a certain order to ask them, that works well in delivering the pathologos problem. Of course, there are times when the philosophical midwife adapts the basic design of the questions to meet the needs of a particular person, and when that happens, the method itself guides the discussion.

Asking questions takes away the need for being a *knower*. The midwife asks the questions, and the person puzzles out the meanings of his or her own answers. This is why *midwife* is such a good term, because he assists in the birth of the idea but doesn't offer answers and interpretations. When a person discovers the answers for himself, it is certain that the answers will be right. Any other person's interpretation will certainly be off base, a little or a lot.

When we set up to do this work, it is an agreement between the midwife and the person to do it. The person goes into the work because he realizes that it's necessary for his growth. He knows there will be obstacles, and as the work proceeds, he will discover the interrelationships of the obstacles. At the same time, as he's doing his own pathologos work, he is learning the method of Philosophical Midwifery.

You can follow each stage of the dialectic here. You can learn more about each stage later in the book.

1. The person begins by stating why they believe they have been able to achieve their goals, or why they have continued harmful behaviors in their life.

2. They give a present example of the difficulties they've had in achieving their goals. The midwife encourages them to give a few more examples, and soon the person realizes that there is a common thread running through all the examples.

3. The midwife asks the person to talk some more about the main ideas, the common thread, and what it means in their life.

4. The midwife encourages the person to explore any difficulty that turns them away from their goal that made them fail. The person will begin to notice that negative thoughts and feelings, and inappropriate actions, have caused their failure.

After the person becomes more familiar with Philosophical Midwifery, the midwife can ask the person to compare these difficulties with their original statement of the problem. After the person understands that they can state their problems, that they can understand them, they can appreciate the difference between their original problem and their difficulties. It may take a while to reach this level of thinking, however.

5. After discussing the role their state of mind has played in their lives, the midwife asks them explore a past scene where they experienced, vividly and intensely, that same state of mind. It may be difficult for the person to associate that state of mind to a particular scene in the past, because it likely has shown up again and again in their lives. In such cases, the midwife can ask if they recognize that state of mind as part of the background of their early life, and to reflect on a time when the state of mind was more intense than usual.

If this fails, the midwife should pursue more examples of the problem in the person's present life, such as at play or at work. More recent scenes may be easier for some people to get into.

There may be times when a person cannot think of any scenes at all, and when this occurs, it is best to recognize it as an obstacle to remembering. Some past episodes have formidable defenses against being remembered, in which case the philosophical midwife may suggest that the dialogue continue at another time or refer the person to a psychotherapist skilled in handling resistances of this kind.

Before making that referral, the midwife may decide to explore the obstacle itself, because it may be a manifestation of the pathologos. The obstacle is also a state of mind, which can be described and discussed just like any past scene. The midwife should be trained to make the determination, or refer the decision to someone who can help, such as a philosophical midwife that trained him or her.

6. As the person reviews the past scenes, ideas and themes that function in and through the family will begin emerge, and the person will begin to see puzzles about their meaning. The midwife asks the subject to face the puzzles and to conclude the meanings of these memories. This begins to reduce the distortions of the past.

7. As the distortions are reduced, the person begins to see the past in a new way.

8. Next, the person can begin to make connections about the past scenes and present scenes, and begin to figure out meanings for these connections.

9. These meanings become solutions or hypotheses that can account for the person's failures in life, and the midwife encourages the person to confirm the hypothesis in everyday life as they pursue their goals.

10. The midwife asks the person to ponder why they accepted and believed the false self-image they got in

the early scenes. By reflecting on this, the person is brought to see that these false beliefs about themselves influenced them and even molded them in some way, and shaped their way of experiencing the world.

11. The discussion takes on a new level when the person sees the interlocking effects of these false beliefs. The midwife helps the person trace the beliefs to significant persons in one's life. The midwife helps the person see how these effects have shaped their life, and even shape the dialogue itself, as the person's responses, recollections, and resistances reflect the

pathologos and even shape the way the person talks about things.

12. Some people may want to take the discussion a step further and reflect on philosophical goals—or self-actualization—and go on to learn the higher functioning of Philosophical Midwifery.

As each stage of the dialectic unfolds, the person will go through a range of states of mind that includes puzzlement, doubt, confusion, fear, surprise, and wonder. The questions that probe through these states are somewhat formal, but in order to help each individual person reach deeper understanding, the midwife must adapt the questions to suit the person's needs. In each encounter, the midwife learns again and again how past scenes generate beliefs and how understanding takes away the power of the pathologos.

Going through these questions will no doubt reveal how *imitation* plays a central role in these problems.

Clearly, authorities and parents in these early scenes appear justified in blocking the child from doing this or that; but at the same time, they also want to deflate or tone down the child's openness and sense of freedom because of the fear of allowing a free expression within the home and in the world.

From these scenes, the child makes a judgment to keep himself from any particular activity, but but he does not recognize that it also puts an end to exhibiting that state of mind of freedom.

The intensity of these scenes lays the foundation for how we think about justice, and forms our ideas of justice and how to appear as someone who knows and cares—and even shapes our idea of love.

Consider this quote from Plato:

"We have, I take it, certain convictions from childhood about the just and the honorable, in which, in obedience and honor to them, we have been bred as children under their parents."

--From Plato's *Republic*, Book VII

Thus, the art of our dialectic exposes these sham ideas of justice and knowing. Our Philosophical Midwifery follows that platonic tradition. It is a dialectic because it is a formal approach to a problem, it has a set of questions it follows, and while they may be adapted to meet the circumstances of the interview, they are, nonetheless, a model, and the questioning model is a dialectic.

The cycle of inquiry, reflecting on our problems, and authenticating in our experience, is the process that brings to light those beliefs. Then they are available for us to judge them true or false. A problem is like a multifaceted gem. We can't get rid of the problem until we explore all the facets and see how they contribute to the whole. Therefore, the number of talks required to eliminate a problem depends on the number of factors involved, and the clarity of the person's seeing.

This process teaches us a new kind of understanding and reasoning, freeing us from what formerly kept us a shadow of what we are. We call it Philosophical Midwifery because it is in the Socratic tradition. In Plato's *Theœtetus*, Socrates describes his art of Philosophical Midwifery.

> *"But the greatest thing about my art is this, that it can test in every way whether the mind of the young man is bringing forth a mere image, an imposture, or a real and genuine offspring."*

Parmenideas of Elea was said to dialogue in this way, according to Proclus, when he helped Socrates himself get rid of false ideas. In Plato's *Symposium*, Socrates describes himself as being initiated into philosophy by a philosophical midwife. From this art of reflecting comes the expression that *the unexamined life is not worth living.*

Dreaming and the Pathologos
The Dream Master

Of all the experiences we have to help us, our dreams can be the most revealing and the most personal. Exploring dreams helps us understand ourselves and our reality, and can be a great resource in overcoming our pathologos problems.

Where do our dreams come from? It's an important question and one we can confidently answer in Philosophical Midwifery. We speak of the source of our dreams as the Dream Master, a profound influence in our entire lives.

The "maker of dreams," the Dream Master, is aware of our personal past—it *must* be— since it uses our past history as the material for our dreams. It artfully selects key images from our past to give us the message of the dream, and it knows just what we have ignored from our waking world, and reminds us of its significance, both now and in the past.

The maker of dreams is awake in our life in a way that we ourselves are not. In this way we, the dreamers, can know that there is something beyond us, something that is yet present to us, something intelligent that works for our personal good and, hence, is providential in its vision. This maker of dreams we call the Dream Master because its mastery is profound in its understanding and most artful in its production.

This is a Philosophical Midwifery approach to dreaming, not a psychological approach, and this is an important distinction. Psychology uses a system of interpretation, while Philosophical Midwifery never interprets, but instead relies on the dreamer's own understanding, so we can see for ourselves how false beliefs are at the root of all our problems. Thus we can test conclusions we reach through this method and verify them when we apply them to our own experience. Thus, exploring each dream takes the form of a structured PM dialogue designed to uncover a person's belief system, and it is a system of reasoning, not interpretation.

After many years of analyzing the content of many people's dreams, I have realized that we are only partly aware, in our waking life, of the problems, failures, and the victories of our waking life. We usually don't realize that dreams play a vital complementary role in our psychic life. And since the rational process of Philosophical Midwifery shows this so clearly, the method is ideal—and important— to use in dream work.

In learning about dreams, we dreamers learn about our personal lives and at the same time, learn a method of analysis that we can use in many ways in our lives. Once the method becomes second nature to dreamers, we apply it to other areas of our lives and learn to anticipate the occurrence of problems, find ourselves more fully aware in our lives, and recognize more fully what we had previously ignored.

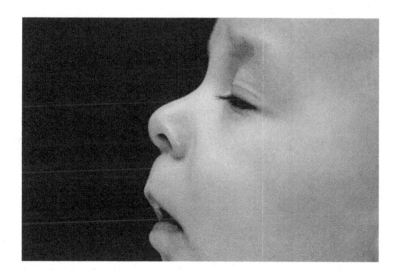

When we begin to use this method, over time, we see that dreams often carry a theme across many dreams, that there are important links between dreams, and that later dreams correct or modify the conclusions we made earlier.

The Dream Master uses metaphors, analogies, images, and narrative to help us understand our pathologos problems, since the failures and successes that we ignore in the waking world become the subjects of the dream. When we analyze our dreams, we see that they have their roots in those beliefs about ourselves that have been formulated in our early youth, those which were never spoken aloud and therefore cannot be recalled—the pathologos.

As we have learned, these beliefs begin in early experiences in our youth, during occasions when families disclose their fundamental and emotionally-held beliefs about life, about ourselves, and about family members. From them, we draw our own conclusions, in private, about ourselves and the nature of reality.

As we have seen, these beliefs are the root cause of our problems because they are *always* false. The family never discusses them, but they live as milieu beliefs and taboos within the family. Invariably, these beliefs were shared when we ourselves were in the state of mind of approaching a success that threatened or challenged the beliefs of the family authorities. Thus, later in life, whenever we face similar situations or states of mind that would threaten those family beliefs, we withdraw and find a solution that preserves or can be reconciled with those family taboos.

As we have seen, we believed these false beliefs because the family authorities gave the appearance of being most caring, genuine and sincere. It appeared that they cared for us so much that they wanted share with us their fundamental convictions. So, rejecting such beliefs would be tantamount to rejecting the authorities (almost always our parents), leaving us to face possible exile and loss of affection. Sadly, though, while these beliefs shape an image of ourselves and our reality, they are, in principle, false and irreconcilable with our highest ideals—the pathologos. The pathologos causes our sense of dissatisfaction and failure in life. When our possible achievements contradict these beliefs, then we experience blocks that either dilute our achievements or that simply cause us to fail.

Our dreams show us these blocks and set them within scenes that show their common elements and structure within the history of our life. Using PM, we can unlock those personal blocks to our achievement of excellence and come to the possibility of leading a more rational—and a more joyful—life.

Dreams and the Pathologos

Because dreams are analogical constructions that use symbols, metaphors, and images, they sometimes seem difficult to understand, and because the Dream Master shows us elements that directly address our pathologos problems, our dreams may sometimes seem hard to deal with. In most traditions, dreams are a pathway to the spiritual life. And our work here offers us this unusual idea: using *understanding* as our way to the life of the spirit—and the path of philosophy is the way to understanding. This makes the philosophical path to spirituality unique and profound among spiritual traditions.

This way of understanding has its roots in the past, but it has been largely forgotten or ignored by most people today. Indeed, *understanding* plays a very modest role in religion and psychology, both of which discount and even trivialize it. Yet it is only the *mind* that can know the mind, and understanding is the doorway to the mind. The fullest expression of this ancient path of understanding is found in the Platonic tradition, and each time it has been given the proper soil, it has flowered into many rebirths in both the East and the West.

Even so, most of us do not think of philosophy and spirituality as having any relationship at all. This is because the study of philosophy has changed during the last few hundred years. Platonic philosophy was traditionally considered a path to spirituality, while the study of philosophy in modern times has turned into reading and discussing various philosophers and their beliefs. Our work here returns to the Platonic view that philosophy is a means to spirituality by finding the truth, not an imposed truth from religion or dogma, but the truth of our lives.

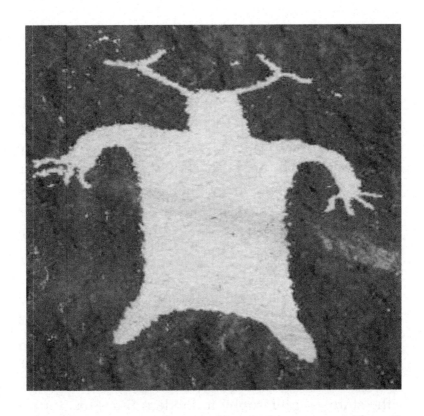

The way we perceive reality is in our minds, of course, and our mind can be awakened through the understanding, so understanding, through the mind, is our path to spirituality. However, the path of understanding in Plato is a twofold dynamic process in that one can only go as high as one has gone deep. To make it work, we face the difficult task of getting rid of our false beliefs about ourselves and about reality.

In Plato, this comes through the study of dreams. He outlines his approach in Book Nine of his *Republic*. Most people don't know that Plato includes dream work, nor do they know about the origin and power of the pathologos. Plato views the philosopher's task as questioning and challenging the believer's loyalty to milieu problems, which he sees as the source of most of our misery.

Why would we hold onto these false beliefs about ourselves? For Plato, the answer lies here: that the child learns by imitation and frames a false self-image. As we have seen, this takes place when the child is open and receptive and when the persuaders of these false beliefs appear most sincere. Then the powerful influences of the family or clan can work their destructive designs on the innocent youth. They mold an image that compels us to compromise our own view of ourselves. These persuaders (sadly our parents most of the time), use praise and blame, intimidation and rewards, and so we go through the process that shapes us so that we resemble and imitate the members of our family, whose own nature was distorted in a similar way.

There are two kinds of influences that bring us to believe false beliefs about ourselves and reality. One is called the milieu and the other pathologos scenes. The milieu is the background beliefs and ways of being of the family that we tend to imitate without the slightest reflection. The pathologos we experiences as thoughts and feelings when we step outside the accepted boundaries that the family, religion, or culture declare as proper. The feelings we experience are strong enough to block and inhibit us from venturing into an area of freedom and creativity. The pathologos expresses the limits of the milieu and together they create the obstacles to our spiritual destiny.

We accepted these false beliefs about our self because the persuaders appeared so believable, since they had to appear as if they sincerely cared and wanted to help us. By appearing virtuous, they create the conditions for vice. We accepted these destructive beliefs with an unwavering and unquestioning loyalty. Thus we gave up our soul to incorrect images that shaped our life, since they formed the model for our existence (and the existence of the members of our family).

If you have read Plato (or if you had to study a little about him in school), you are probably familiar with his Allegory of the Cave, where images are projected on the wall of the cave. These are the shadows of virtue, and they are taken for real by the believers. They are the images of the pathologos.

We have long forgotten the beginnings of our pathologos, but our dreams play the pathologos images before us and keep alive the conflict born from the compromise that gave birth to these images. If we do not challenge the images and the pathologos, they are like daydreams that go over and over what should have been avoided. They bring out the worst of us, the tyrant, to live a life that is a nightmare of horror. Our daydreams use images of ourselves that we identify with and spin out the inherent drama within them so that we can learn the folly of believing what is false about ourselves.

The Dream Maker, the craftsman of our dreams, reminds us that what we believe to be real is false. In understanding our dreams, we can learn about how we believe what is false about ourselves, and we also come to understand the language of the dream world. Plato explains the need to study dreams so that in discovering what has blocked us in our past, we discover the roots of our problem and what has created the tragic consequences in our present. In doing so, we can regain control of our destiny through understanding our dreams, and this frees us to begin to understand reality.

Your mind is your best friend and ally, since it crafts our dreams to give us an astonishing understanding of ourselves for our growth and development. You can study your dreams and learn about yourself, knowing that your existence is intelligible.

Dreamwork itself is nothing new. Freud and Jung introduced the systematic study of dream interpretation as a psychotherapeutic method to Europe. Yet even before that, in classical times, dreams were treated as a form of divination, and were considered important to study. Physicians often looked to the dreams of a patient prior to offering any treatment for an illness. Dreams play a significant role in Homer's *Iliad* as well in Aeschylus' *Persians*. Plato, in Book Nine of his *Republic*, says that to the degree one is indifferent to the study of dreams, it is to that degree that the irrational desires dominate one's life. In the extreme, a tyrant acts out his daydreams, which becomes for his subjects a hideous nightmare. Thus, for Plato the antidote for the fantasy life driven by contrary desires is the study of one's dreams.

I began working with dreams in Philsophical Midwifery when I realized that the problems we consciously choose to discuss might not be central to our own destiny, while the content of dreams presents a deeper level of personal struggles that are for the most part unsuspected. Soon I added the study of daydreams when I saw that daydreams contain not only self-images that maintain a person's problem, but offer keys to uncover their roots.

Daydreams

The idea that dreams may provide a key to understanding unsuspected beliefs that lie at the root of our problems has only recently gained a degree of acceptance. Daydreams by contrast have not been studied as they should be, even though it is obvious that daydreams and fantasies are often dress rehearsals that may be acted out to some degree in life. Daydreams can divert our attention and create tangents to our goals. We find them immediately compelling; we identify with them wholeheartedly. The drama in the daydream is as familiar as are the scenes and characters they contain. However, most people don't recognize daydreams as having vital links to our fundamental problems, nor do we suspect that they help maintain our problems.

Over the years, in our workshops and meditation retreats, we have focused on the kind of daydreams that are similar in structure to our personal problems, exploring these using Philosophical Midwifery. From these past explorations, we know that the thoughts and images that erupt and block our effort to achieve our significant goals are directly linked to the drama of our dreams. Adding daydreams has made the work even more effective.

Throughout our day, our thoughts and images impose themselves over whatever we are doing. At these times, they distract us from what we are doing and disrupt our attention, but at other times they may be a kind of inner whisper that attends our doings. There are times when they command our attention and demand to be heard and heeded, but just why they come when they do is has mostly remained a mystery.

However, even though we may know little about them, we have learned some things about daydreams. They can be regarded as fragments that remind us that there is something about our present moment that points to things in our life which are still unresolved and which need our deepest attention. They bring us to reflect upon our past and our hopes and fears of the future. They can be regarded as being seed-like, in that when nurtured by fantasy and watered by desire, they either help produce a harvest of what we have reached out for and desired, or they become like entangling vines that choke off our noblest ideals.

Clearly, studying our daydreams can give us an important additional way of understanding our problems. Daydreams have an inherent drama linked to them that has a commanding presence and meaning. Of course, there are many kinds of daydreams; here we distinguish them into five kinds.

The first of the five is a daydream we voluntarily enter into. Another kind is the daydream that completes some story, and these are symbolic dream projections. A third kind we enter in order to pursue our own ideal, a desired goal or wish. A fourth kind includes tangents that take one from some appointed task. The fifth we call the koan-like daydream, because they are recollections of past scenes that often surface, challenging us to discover alternative ways of dealing with this past scene. They persist until we find that our own limited self-image was what blocked a better way of dealing with the situation.

Of these five—the planned, symbolic dream projections, the ideal, the tangent, and the koan-like— we used the ideal and the tangent daydream for workshop explorations to compare with dreams. As workshop participants were guided through these daydreams, we noted that there is a special moment in them that is important to recognize. When we enter the daydream, we forget everything else going on, so we can say that we forget about our everyday life until the daydream is over and we awaken to our everyday reality. For this reason, a daydream is like a dream, since it is a kind of falling asleep and later waking up. It is forgetting one world and entering another. Since the world one enters into is a fiction, it is a pure example of a kind of ignorance.

Just as entering a daydream is a kind of ignorance, so too coming out of it is a kind of knowing. To believe that you are what you are *not* is ignorance, just as rejecting any false image of the self, for even a brief time, is enlightenment. Here in this simple episode of life, a daydream, we have the major issues of philosophy, because to identify the self with an image in a daydream, a dream, or any kind of identification with anything, is to form a false belief about ourselves. Our work in philosophy is to challenge these false beliefs about the self and to discover how we accepted them.

As we have seen, Philosophical Midwifery brings to the surface unsuspected false beliefs about our self, pathologos beliefs, which we learned in our youth. Daydreams preserve these false beliefs and maintain their destructive effect in the present. To bring help us see the relationships between dreams and daydreams, I crafted what I call the "tangent daydream." I asked workshop participants to record their dreams and to voluntarily enter into these tangent daydreams in order to directly learn the way the mind works.

Here is how we did it. Workshop participants were asked to imagine repeatedly numbers from 1 to 10 appearing before them. During this experience, they were also asked to discover where the numbers were coming from and what was watching the numbers. They were instructed to pay attention to any thoughts or images that took them away from the task, and we asked if they would consider sharing these daydreams at the workshop sessions. We would compare and contrast these daydreams with their dreams.

As for dreams, workshop participants were asked to make an audio recording of their dreams as soon as possible after waking and then transcribe the recordings so that they could be read out loud and discussed at the workshop. Participants also asked compared the content of dreams that were recorded soon after awaking with dreams that they wrote down after a few hours, and further, with a remembered verbal report of their dreams.

We compared these at the workshop. Workshop members were surprised at how differently they remembered the dream, when they tried to recall it later in the day, than how it was when they recorded immediately after awakening. After hearing both the transcribed recording and the written recollection, we all noticed that the key terms that had played such a major role in the analysis were present and more evident in the recording of the dream than the written report and the least accurate was the verbal report. In comparing these various kinds of dream reports, the further we were from the transcribed recording, the more the key terms were either missing or the language used to communicate them was less vital and accurate.

When we try to remember dreams later in the day, we fall into the trap of interpretation, including adding and subtracting dream content. In our workshops, participants usually work from the transcribed recording. When participants relate their dream, I record the content with drawings and actual images and words from the dream, using an easel, and then I review and analyze them. Those who offered their dreams and/or their daydreams for discussion do so voluntarily.

After the workshops, I ask participants for written feedback to a series of questions in the form of a field survey. When asked about the explorations of the dreams and daydreams at the workshop, people wrote that they appreciated knowing the relationship between dreams and daydreams, and that our dreaming life is intelligible and helpful to us. In particular, they appreciated having a model for analysis, something they can follow and understand.

Most people regard daydreams as trivial, even taboo. However, after our analysis at the workshop, participants appreciated the insights they gained from daydreams and further reported that they were having less daydreams since they did this work. When they do have daydreams, they think of them as meaningful and worth studying. One said, "My whole fantasy world is in danger. Hallelujah!"

After the workshop, they appreciate the depth that daydreams offer and are more conscious of them and see them as "nurturing" and their messages as meaningful.

Dreamwork is sometimes difficult at first, because it includes similes, metaphors, and analogical thinking. In contrast, modern education teaches us to explore ideas using inductive thinking, drawing conclusions from studying what we observe. The language of dreams, however, is in *symbols* that we need to study as similes, metaphors, and analogies. It embraces scenes from our present and past, it creates bridges that can overcome the gap of forgetfulness, and in a grand sweep, and it presents our present life's struggles in terms of patterns learned in our youth, thereby leaving an open avenue to the future. To make connections between present and past is to find analogies (comparisons that cross over between one thing and another), similarities in the language, images, and states of mind, and so the philosophical midwife needs skill in this type of comparative analysis.

These messages from our mind often seem very strange, so we must learn a new way of understanding the meanings in the language of dreams and daydreams. We call it the functional way of understanding, a new way to find the meaning behind the images, similes, and analogies. These messages from our dreams and daydreams are allegories to contemplate for our soul's enlightenment. Our mind communicates to us in a very sophisticated and profound way, so to grasp its meaning, we need to learn this profound way of communicating. Since our mind functions for our personal benefit, we can see that there is a goodness that flows to each of us in a personal and natural way through the messages from the mind.

When we are open and receptive to these messages from our mind, when we begin to pay attention to them, we begin to see that these messages will allow us that most excellent result, to "know thyself." This idea is ancient and timely at the same time, for providence is available to all, to benefit anybody who will receive it. The idea of providence itself was understood in classical times as the nature of goodness, which freely flows to those receptive to it, with an infinite power and capability of benefiting all. For those who wish to see the ancient roots of this concept, Proclus in his *Commentary on Plato's Parmenides* beautifully presents a full description of providence through the 24 categories of the dialectic.

The Dream Master

Most of us agree that we fully identify with our dreams and that we are swept up in the drama of our dreams. Most of us also feel we don't really know *why* we dream or how our dreams relate to our life as a whole. Since our dreams show an astonishing artistry, a compelling vividness, and a deep knowledge of each of our personal dramas that are rich with meaning, we realize that there is a master of dreams who possesses an incredible wisdom — that comes to us for our benefit. And that would have to be true over all time and for all who have the capacity to dream.

Do You Need a Guru?

Much dream analysis hinges on the interpretations of a therapist or a guru. Philosophical Midwifery, however, must have no therapist, priest, or guru role. The midwife is a helpful assistant, operating as a peer, not an authority. This model, again, originates in Plato. In outlining how fellow philosophers should relate to one another, he says that together they are like one man, a Hellenic. Even though this ideal is difficult to achieve, it is nonetheless important to strive for it. As an example, in a workshop held at the Esalen Institute in California, we found that when one

146

member expressed her insight, others' thoughts were in total agreement. "It was as if I only heard one person speaking. Every dream and daydream was something I could identify with and understand. Day after day, I was struck with this idea that there is a oneness I never thought could ever be."

In your analysis of both dreams and daydreams, you do not need any special language nor a special mode of interpretation. You just ask the same kind of questions in each case and draw from the person what the dream and daydream means. This is the same process that we use in PM generally and again, this draws from the Platonic tradition. The problems we have were learned in our youth and can be unlearned once we realize the folly of the learning, that is, when we reflect on the conditions that brought us to believe something about ourselves that was false and continues to be false. This work is not psychology; neither does it have anything in common with those religions that believe that man is in a state of sin.

More about the Dream Master

The idea of a maker of dreams can be hard for some to accept. Here are some ideas that make it easier to grasp. First, the source of these communications, these dreams, must participate in goodness, have a power capable of extending its activities over time, and be amazingly effective in its communications. To possess this kind of knowledge for each dreamer throughout time leads to the conclusion that the source must possess some kind of map capable of charting the spiritual direction of mankind, or for a species capable of dreaming. It must possess knowledge vast in its scope and precise in its expression, since it reveals the unique circumstances of each dreamer to fulfill their most vital goals. And it must possess a masterful craftsmanship of creating symbols, similes, metaphors, and analogies that are so artful that dreamers readily identify with the images and drama.

Whatever the Dream Master is, this source of our dreams and daydreams has an intimate knowledge of ourselves. To function in this way, the Dream Master must possess an incredible diagnostic ability to understand us, day by day, so it can give us dreams that fit our higher goals and the entangling problems we face in securing them. This kind of knowledge must include a keen watchfulness over our day-to-day struggles as well as over our entire life journey. This reflects a spiritual dimension, for it brings together our past and present, freeing us from past mistakes and opening us to grander participation in mindfulness.

In addition, these communications possess such a profound depth of meaning that while they are unique to each dreamer, they also share a common direction and are understandable to others. Philosophical Midwifery gives us a common language and a way of exploring we can share. Since the dreams and daydreams are in the form of images, ideas and states of mind, or feeling states that can be understood as metaphors, similes and analogies to our own life, we can practice and study this method endlessly, to help ourselves and to help others.

This kind of thinking contradicts the common modern view that "everything is relative" and that you can't really understand things. Those who share the experiences and reflections of Philosophical Midwifery may participate in intelligence not actually resident in themselves. Finally we can experience the kind of change we may have been looking for during our life, bringing inner harmony, a higher logos (or intelligible principle), something we can depend on, be guarded by, and be benefited by.

This type of work is open to all in our homes. What we need to know, we can discover for ourselves. There is no need for any distant pilgrimages, no sacrifice of what is yours, only dedication to truth and a thirst to know if we can verify for ourselves that we are part of a caring and intelligible cosmos. The realization is not some distant goal, nor a faith-based hope, because we have within ourselves a way to transform ourselves.

What we gain is not a moment of glory nor some passing intense experience, but a growth in our own profound kind of understanding. The sense of isolation and being separate from one another is ended. With the growth in understanding ourself, we know we can be open to sharing and learning about someone else. In the rejection of the old self-images comes a new openness to a maturity that treasures integrity and excellence.

What emerges is the idea of Man that outshines those religious ideals, goes beyond the scholar, far beyond the martyrs of Islam, or the soldiers of Christ. We can take a hard look at these old images of man and ask if they do justice to man's dream of self-mastery through the cultivation of understanding. We are guided by images, and if the images cannot match our noblest efforts to understand ourselves, they are flawed and useless in our development.

If you have children, it may be worthwhile to think about teaching them about dream and daydream study. There is an old adage that says you can't have a dream you can't understand. To use plays and stories, programs and video productions to teach these ideals would be a doorway to introduce these ideas into our culture. We can see this in C.S. Lewis' *Chronicles of Narnia, The Last Battle,* since he concludes that the tale itself is an allegory: "It's all in Plato, all in Plato, bless me, what do they teach them in their Schools? "

Where Do We Go From Here?

We can emerge free with a crown of integrity once we come to realize that we must not only challenge injustices, but also cultivate and nurture the truth that lies within us. However, to reach this truth, we need to understand why we have hidden the sight of injustice from ourselves. Primal injustice is something we have learned from those who raised us, for they, unknowingly, sought to protect us from what they themselves feared. We learned this fear. It undermines our confidence in acting against injustice because we have suffered it ourselves.

To free ourselves from our own folly, we need to discover how we came to fear freedom. We need only to recall that in our own youthful days, we stepped across the boundary of what was acceptable and learned the price we pay for breaking that taboo. But we learned more than just keeping within the bounds of safety, since that simple step into freedom offered authorities the chance to play out their image of power over us. In those scenes, we were convinced that we lacked the ability to judge what was true, so we came to believe the act that authorities played out, since they appeared so knowing and sincere.

Thus, when we encounter situations analogous to those early scenes, we experience similar states of mind and hold ourselves back rather than face condemnation similar to what we earlier had experienced. We become cowards and fear that freedom that once was the hallmark of our earlier years, and so we pay dearly for our obeisance.

When we were young, when we surrendered our freedom, we gained membership within the clan and picked up a role to play out within the tribe. With that surrender, we came to identify with the irrational forces that oppose the mind. We have followed the beliefs of the clan with unreflective certainty and demand the sacrifice, punishment, exile and death of those who threaten these beliefs, in a form of tribal loyalty. Whenever we in turn get into a position of power, we imitate what has been done to us and pass on to one another the injustices we have suffered.

Fearing freedom of expression sanctifies and preserves blind authority and stunts the growth of maturity; it keeps those who might have challenged authority as immature children. The fear of freedom is the fear that one's own mind cannot be trusted to bring about integrity in one's own life.

However, we don't need to remain trapped in this way. Philosophical Midwifery offers us the tools to break free of our lifelong patterns, regain our personal freedom, and take the lifelong journey to personal excellence.

Why We Are Here

Whatever you say,
you know you said it.
Knowing you said it
makes you different
than before you said it
because
having put it into words,
you risked being wrong,
but you expressed it.
Now you understand
what you said and
you are shaped by what you said.
For you see through
your understanding like
you speak through your words and
that becomes a way of being yourself.
So, express what is within you and
share what you see,
for we are here to see and to share what we see.

Pierre Grimes Biography

Military Record

Army Service: 36th Infantry, 142nd Regiment,
1st Battalion S-2 Intelligence section.
Participated in six campaigns, two invasions.
Received Purple Heart, Bronze Star with an Oak Leaf
Cluster.
Received Unit Presidential Citation for Heroism with
an Oak Leaf Cluster for the Battle of Anzio, Italy and
for Selestat, France.

Education

St. John's College
Annapolis, Maryland
1948-52
San Francisco State University
San Francisco, California
1953-4
University of the Pacific
San Francisco, California
M.A. and Ph.D.
Comparative Studies
1955-60
New School of Social Research
New York, New York
Post Doctorate Studies, 1961-3

Teaching

University of the Pacific
San Francisco, California
Lecturer in Comparative Philosophy
Ancient and Modern Philosophy
1955-60
Orange Coast College
Costa Mesa, California
Lecturer in Philosophy
Ancient and Modern Philosophy
1964-66
Golden West College
Huntington Beach, California
Professor of Philosophy
1966-2004
Esalen Institute
Big Sur, California
Five day Workshops
1985 to Present (winter and summer)
University of Philosophical Research
Los Angeles, California
Professor, Classical Philosophy
1990 - present
Holmes Institute Graduate School
Los Angeles, California
Professor of Philosophy, Hellenic Philosophy
1999-present

Research
Motivation Dynamics
Design and Motivation Studies
Mohegan Lake, New York

Grimes and Associates:
Research through Dialogues
Client list includes AT&T, Young and Rubicam, Santa Ana, California and Huntington Beach, California (confidential list of studies provided upon request)

Books and Publications

Philosophical Midwifery: The Art of Delivering Ideas, Dionysius Publications, Garden Grove, CA 92645, 1989.

Being, The One: A Philosophical Dialogue, Westminster Press, Westminster, CA, 1976, reprinted by Opening Mind Press, 1995.

"Is It All Relative?" A Play on Plato's *Theatetus,* 1st Ed 1989, Dionysius Publications, 6th edition, Hyparxis Press, Costa Mesa, CA, 1995.

A New Paradigm for Understanding Problems: Philosophical Midwifery, the Art of Delivering False Beliefs and the Validation of the Dialectic as a Mode of Rational Psychotherapy, co-authored with Dr. Regina Uliana, Hyparxis Press, Costa Mesa, CA 1998.

"The Art of Delivering Oneself of False Beliefs", in 2 parts, *New Perspectives*, July, 1994, p. 26 and Nov/Dec, 1994, p. 10.

Return of the Gods, five part dialogue-play, currently being reviewed for publication.

The Philosophical Path of Dreams and Daydreams, Lulu Press, 2007.

8,000 Years of Wisdom, by Michelle Abadie and Mike Cast, including a contribution by Pierre Grimes, 2009, compiled and published in the UK.

Philosophical Perspectives from Pierre Grimes and Opening Mind Writers, An Anthology of Articles and Reviews originally published in *New Perspectives: A Journal of Conscious Living,* compiled by Allan Hartley, 1997-2008, Lulu Press 2009

Five Philosophical Dialogues, Lulu Press, 2009

The Way of the Logos, LULU Press, 2011

Journal Articles:

"Philosophical Midwifery," *APPA Journal,* Vol. 3 No. 3, Oct. 2008.

"Homer and the Struggle for Excellence," *Journal of the American Philosophical Practitioners Association,* Vol. 1 No. 1, Routledge, Taylor and Francis Group, Milton Park, Abingdon, UK, March 2005.

"Philosophical Practice," *APPA Journal*: Vol.1 No.1 (2005)

"Alcibiades: A Dialogue Utilizing the Dialectic as a mode of Psychotherapy for Alcoholism", *Yale Journal: Quarterly Journal of Studies on Alcoho*l, 22, 1961.

"Vinodorus:: A Dialogue Exploring a Frame of Reference for Dialectic as a Mode of Psychotherapy in the Treatment of Alcoholism." *Rutgers U. Press Quarterly Journal of Studies on Alcohol* 27, 1966.

Various articles in journal of the Noetic Society, Inc., *The Hellenic Chariot,* 1990-1995.

Computer Program

To Artemis: The Challenge to Know Thyself, (1989). A computer program by Pierre Grimes on Hypercard for Macintosh designed to guide users through over 400 thoughtfully structured questions for self-analysis. Now available through the internet: www.noeticsociety.org

A workbook based on the *To Artemis* Program was developed by Joseph Grimes, 1992.

Professional Memberships
American Philosophical Practice Association
Board Member, Faculty Member
Certified in Client Counseling

American Society of Philosophical Counseling and Psychotherapy, Board member

American Philosophical Practitioners Association, Board member, Staff Member, Certified Client Counseling

Golden West College
Emeritus Professor of Philosophy

Positions Held

The Noetic Society, Inc.,Founder and President

Opening Mind Academy, Noetic Society, Inc. For the Study of the Platonic Tradition and Dialectic.
Huntington Beach, California and Costa Mesa, California

Regular Friday night meetings:
 8:30 PM to 10PM dream studies and
10:00 PM to midnight explorations of various classical philosophical works, centered around the Platonic Tradition.

Generated over 100 DVD's on Philosophy and Philosophical Midwifery, www.noeticsociety.org or www.academyofplatonicstudies.com (many available on YouTube)

Academy of Platonic Studies, President, Director of Studies, 1992 to present 2009
Waldorf School of Orange County

Board Member 1990-1994

Conference Participation
"A Validation of the Grimes Dialectic as a Mode of Psychotherapy," 94th Annual Conference American Psychological Association, Washington D.C., USA August, 1986

Lecture and Demonstration of Philosophical Midwifery, The Philosophical Counseling Workshop Conference International Association of Philosophical Counseling & Enquiry, London, England, November, 1996

"The Emergence of the Pathologos in Dreams," Association for the Study of Dreams, 71st Annual American Philosophical Association Conference, Berkeley, California, July, 1996

"Defining Philosophical Midwifery," American Society of Philosophical Counseling & Psychotherapy, 72nd Annual American Philosophical Association Conference, Berkeley, California, April, 1997

"False Beliefs: The Pathologos in Philosophical Midwifery," American Society of Philosophical Counseling and Psychotherapy, American Philosophical Association, Pittsburgh, Pennsylvania, April, 1997

"A Study of Philosophical Midwifery and a Demonstration," Third International Conference on Philosophical Counseling, New York, New York, August, 1997

"The Moral Crisis in the Exploration of Philosophical Midwifery," Paideia: Twentieth World Congress of Philosophy, Boston, Massachusetts, August, 1998

"Symmetry and the Origin of the Pathologos in Philosophical Midwifery," With Barbara Stecker, Fifth International Conference of Philosophy in Practice, Wadham College, Oxford, England, July, 1999

"Philosophical Midwifery: a New Paradigm," VIII International Symposium on Philosophy and Culture, Russian Academy of Sciences, St. Petersburg, Russia, September, 2000

"A New Paradigm: A Hyperspace Model for Dialectical Philosophical Practice," Fourth Conference of Science and Consciousness, Albuquerque, New Mexico, April, 2002

"The Process of Alienation and Transition in Dialectical Philosophical Practice," presented by Dr. Regina Uliana, Eighth Conference of the International Society for the Study of European Ideas (ISSEI), Wales, United Kingdom, July, 2002

"Transcendentalism and Pragmatism in Dialectical Philosophical Practice," American Society for Philosophy, Counseling, and Psychotherapy, 77th Annual American Philosophical Association, San Francisco, California, March, 2003

"Introduction and Demonstration of Philosophical Midwifery," Canadian Society for Philosophical Practice, University of St. Paul, Ottawa, Canada, September, 2003

"The Dialectical Philosophical Practice: A New Paradigm for Understanding Human Problems," XXIst World Congress of Philosophy, Istanbul, Turkey, August, 2003

"Homer and the Struggle for Excellence," International Association for Greek Philosophy, Athens, Greece, First World Olympic Congress of Philosophy, March 2004

"Rational Structure of Pathologos Problems," University of Liverpool Philosophy Conference Keynote Speaker, London, 2006

"The structure of analogy in book six of Plato's Republic," School of Economic Science, London, 2006

"The Necessity of Dream Analysis in the Philosopher's Art in Plato's Republic," The First Prometheus Trust Conference, Maidencroft Farm, Glastonbury, Somerset, England, 2006

"Introduction to Philosophical Midwifery: through a DVD presentation of dialectic applied to a dream and daydreams by Pierre Grimes," IX International

Conference on Philosophical Practice, Carloforte, 2008, with Dr. Regina Uliana

"The Parallel Structure of the Pathologos and the Human Cell and its relation to Cancer," Tenth Annual Meeting of the APPA at City College of New York, 2009

"Plato's Myth of Er and its relationship to Dream study in Plato's Republic," Three-day study at the Krotona School of Metaphysics, Ojai, California, 2010

"Tibetan Book of the Dead and Plato's Myth of Er," Five-day workshop at the Krotona School of Metaphysics, Ojai, California, 2010

"The Way of the Logos: The Cube as a Way of Understanding Plato's Parmenides and the Unity of World Religions." Three-day guided meditation/study at the Institute of Mental Physics, Joshua Tree, CA, 2011

Religions:
I was given the dharma name of Hui-An by one who became to be the living 78th Patriarch of the Korean Zen Chogye order, Myo-Bong, who personally supported my unique work and teachings, including the practice I learned with him.

About Cathy Wilson

helpertouch@gmail.com

Cathy Wilson is a teacher, writer and artist living in Southern California.

Made in the USA
Coppell, TX
19 December 2022

90077274R00095